You, Me, and a Few Billion More

Jessma Oslin Blockwick

ABINGDON

Nashville

YOU, ME, AND A FEW BILLION MORE

Copyright © 1979 by Abingdon

Library of Congress Cataloging in Publication Data

BLOCKWICK, JESSMA O, 1922-
You, me, and a few billion more.   304. 6
                                                 B651 y

Bibliography: p. 126
1. Population—Moral and religious aspects.
2. Population policy—Moral and religious aspects.
3. Birth control—Moral and religious aspects.
I. Title.
HQ766.2.B56   301.32   79-170

ISBN 0-687-46759-4

MANUFACTURED BY THE PARTHENON PRESS AT
NASHVILLE, TENNESSEE, UNITED STATES OF AMERICA

Contents

To Tom, Penelope, Craig

CHAPTER 1

It's a Matter of People

⁎⁎ María kept her head bent low over her sewing as she tried desperately to think what to do. She had been so lucky to find this work; it seemed as though the children would have enough food to eat for the first time since Ramón had abandoned them all. Now she was pregnant again and so very tired. She thought of the five children in their tar-paper shack taking care of themselves while she did the sewing. Would nine-year-old Luis, the oldest, be able to handle a new baby too? It was too much to ask, but she could not afford to stay at home with them, and the government would not help. Her eyes filled with tears, but she made her decision: She would have to go to old Alberta for an abortion.

⁎⁎ Ahmad tossed and turned in his bed, unable to go to sleep. Resentment and anger seemed to swell in his brain till it pressed on his very skull. The memory had come again of the day in the railroad station when he had been pushed into the vasectomy tent and sterilized. He was only twenty-five and had been married just one year. How could his wife respect him when he could not give her any more children, and they had only one, a daughter? Who would there be to take care of them when he could no longer work? How could such a thing happen? The questions pounded over and over in his mind, but there was no answer—

5

*** Lois actually sang as she drove the car home from the doctor's office. Now that her pregnancy was confirmed, an overwhelming sense of happiness filled her. Of course, they hadn't planned to have another child since everything was so expensive these days. And she had faithfully used contraceptives, but she was secretly glad of the failure. They would manage somehow. She loved babies so much!

*** José shivered in the cold night air, partly from the chill, partly from fear and excitement. Then the guide was there, telling everyone how to move, how to lie whenever they saw lights, sharing his long-practiced skills in getting over the U.S. border. Then they were off, silent now. José tried to think not of being caught but of the money he might make in the United States that could be sent back to his wife and children. There were six of them and another on the way, and no work for him at home. If he did not get across tonight, he knew that he would keep trying. There was nothing else to do.

*** Susie's eyes sparkled as she looked at the beautiful new car in the driveway. How could she ever thank her mom and dad for this sixteenth birthday present? Now she could go to movies and stores on her own, even to the beach; not have to be driven around by them like a baby. Now she could return the favors many of her friends had done for her since they got their own cars earlier. Oh, life was going to be wonderful now!

Here is the world population problem at the micro level, the level of people. For though we usually hear population discussed in terms of statistics, of billions of people, the total cumulates from decisions made and actions taken by millions of individuals and couples. The most profound human emotions surround the decisions about and the actual birth of a baby, ranging from the purest joy to the deepest anguish. Yet these deeply personal matters are shaped by many forces outside the individual.

What we know as the population crisis is not simply a matter of the large number of children the Marías and the Josés are having, but also a matter of the high consumption of resources by the Susies and the Loises. The crisis is also compounded of questions of where people live and where they move, of cultural and religious patterns, and of many other sociological, political, and geographic factors.

In the sixties and early seventies, there was a great spate of articles and books on the population crisis, about the same time the environmental movement was becoming popular. Every study group had its population program. It was an "in" kind of crisis, the kind for which Americans seem to have a voracious appetite—full of doomsday overtones yet not seeming to be immediately threatening to our own comfortable life-style. After that subject seemed sufficiently dealt with, we moved on to the food crisis and the energy crisis, with an occasional look at the New Economic Order proposals or prospects for nuclear warfare.

Still, whether or not we have turned our attention elsewhere, none of the questions raised has been solved. Almost every aspect of the lives of all of us will be increasingly affected by the silent, rapid growth of human population in ways it is not now possible to anticipate as world population doubles, triples, or more in the next one hundred years.

Clearly, we need to take a more concerted look at these population issues and at what they really have to do with us as individuals, as American citizens, and as Christians concerned with justice in the world and with a human level of living for all people.

Since people have always had babies—and many women (or couples) are having fewer babies today than women (or couples) uscd to have—what has changed to make this such a crisis situation? Is it a temporary condition that will solve itself in time? If there is a crisis, why isn't it just a matter of people "over there" having more babies than they can take care of? Is there really much we in the United States can or should do on the population front?

Those are some of the questions this book will seek to examine, along with matters of individual motivations, of national and international policy, and of ethical questions facing us as we make personal choices and as our nation makes political choices in this area of concern.

The whole matter does begin, at least, with numbers. The statistics, though oft repeated, are staggering and therefore hard to grasp. In our own twentieth century, world population will have multiplied about four times, from 1.6 billion at the beginning of the century to 6.2 billion at the close. We begin to appreciate how much this rate has accelerated when we realize that from the time of Christ up to the beginning of this century, world population grew only a little more than six times. Untold millenia had passed before humankind totaled the some 250 million living on the earth when the Christian era began—little more than the present population of the United States.

The rate of population growth depends, simply, on how many more people are born each year than the number who die each year. In our modern era, many more infants are surviving, and death rates in general are declining sharply. The result: rapid population growth. The recent and current rates are unprecedented in human history and obviously cannot be sustained for very long. The question is not whether but how the growth rate is to be lowered and then stabilized. Will it happen automatically without special effort as humankind adjusts to new circumstances? Will it be by rational and humane acts? or by tragedy and catastrophe?

Fertility as a Blessing

The growth rate can be cut either by a rise in the death rate or by a decline in the birthrate. The search is on for ways to bring about the latter in an intentional manner. This question of restraining procreation as a deliberate policy is an entirely new one to confront the human race. For most of history, the concern has been for there to be enough people to ensure survival of the human race, and every force in society united to encourage the bearing of many children. There was always need for more hands, as many as could come along, first for hunting and gathering food, later for clearing the land and tilling the fields. There was an empty world to use—and to fill!

From a very early age, a child was useful as a producer, not simply as a consumer. The small child could tend and feed animals or gather firewood or help in picking fruits and berries. The community was so small that every person added to the group's strength.

The birth of each child, therefore, was an occasion for rejoicing for the whole community. More times than not, the joy turned to sorrow, for most of the babies died early in their lives. Natural hazards constantly surrounded them. There was little protection against disease, and famine was frequent.

Very early, therefore, fertility came to be seen as one of the most precious gifts the gods could bestow, and among the most important religious rites were those that sought to placate the gods and induce them to grant fertility both to women and to the earth itself. The great Mother, symbol of the earth's fertility, was worshiped under many names, among them Cybele, Ishtar, Astarte, Isis, Demeter, Ceres.

The Israelites frequently strayed from Yahweh to bow down before the gods of other peoples, in part because of their practices of fertility rites and cult prostitution.

The Israelites did what was wrong in the eyes of the Lord, and worshipped the Baalim. They forsook the Lord, their fathers' God who had brought them out of Egypt, and went after other gods, gods of the races among whom they lived; they bowed down before them and provoked the Lord to anger; they forsook the Lord and worshipped the Baal and the Ashtaroth. (Judg. 2:11-12)

These were both fertility cults, and the prophets inveighed against them, for Yahweh was the true source of fruitfulness.

Some of the most beautiful language of the psalms sings of the blessing of fruitfulness:

> Sons are a gift from the Lord
>   and children a reward from him.
> Like arrows in the hand of a fighting man
>   are the sons of a man's youth.
> Happy is the man
>   who has his quiver full of them;
> such men shall not be put to shame
>   when they confront their enemies in court.
>   (Psalm 127:3-5)

In the early days of the Christian faith, there was an interval in this stress on procreation because of the expectation that judgment day and Christ's second coming were imminent. As that expectation faded, the Christian Church renewed its stress on procreation, an emphasis it shared with other world religions.

These religious beliefs undergirded cultural and political pressures that encouraged fertility. In spite of this, the growth line of human population crept upward, with occasional frightening lurches downward. In the fourteenth century, the plague spread from Constantinople through-out Europe, and it has been estimated that perhaps three-fourths of the population of Europe and Asia was killed before the disease ran its course. In the middle of the sixteenth century, Britain probably had half a million fewer inhabitants than it had had two centuries earlier when the plague began.[1]

The Hundred Years' War added to the devastation in Europe. It is not hard to understand why all powerful elements in society were united in impressing upon women the necessity to bear many children. The very survival of humanity itself—or at least one's own people—might be at stake.

The Population Curve Turns Upward

Gradually, modernizing trends and new technologies began to overcome some of humankind's ancient scourges in the Western nations. Cities expanded, and urban life was less harsh. There was a growing body of knowledge concerning health practices, nutritional requirements, and sanitation. Agricultural technology improved, as well as communication and transportation, so that food could more easily be moved and distributed as needed. As a result, more babies began to survive their infancy and to live to have children of their own. After all the ages of uncertainty, the population curve turned firmly upward.

Observing this trend, Thomas Malthus, near the end of the eighteenth century, speculated that poverty and starvation on a great scale would be unavoidable because population would increase faster than the means of subsistence could expand. There was a flurry of attention to his ideas for a while, but growing prosperity and optimism led to a general discounting of his theory. Food production expanded rapidly, the industrial plants began to pour forth many goods that made life more comfortable, and science and technology promised an even better life for the future.

Under these comparatively beneficent conditions, the

death rate continued to decline in the West. After an interval of time, the birthrate also began to go down. Parents had more assurance that the babies were going to live; and for the growing number of urban dwellers, children were consumers longer and were therefore more expensive to raise. The decline in fertility did not come very fast, for there was growing employment opportunity in the new industries, and others could move on to the vast expanses of the colonies. In North America particularly, the enormous plains seemed to have space for all who could come. People were needed to clear and till the soil to feed the settlers as well as the exploding populations of Europe. About 40 million immigrants sailed from Europe to North and South America during this expansionist period. Others went to Australia and Africa.

The growing spirit of nationalism meant that social pressures continued to support the large-family ideal; for before the advent of modern weapons, the size of an army determined the nation's power. This political reality was undergirded by the teachings of religions that limiting procreation was a terrible sin.

Even as these pressures continued, the desires and attitudes of individuals regarding family size began to change as they perceived their personal needs. People yearned for effective means of controlling their fertility, a controversial desire that had little outlet for public discussion and expression.

Here we need to step back in time to note that a yearning to limit births, to some degree, has been identifiable throughout all the ages of human history. Running counter to all the pronatalist forces, there was a very personal and largely sub rosa desire to control fertility. Women sickened and aged and died young under the burden of continual childbearing—and they knew it. Husbands too were sometimes burdened by the demands of large families.

Courtesans and their lovers did not want the interference of child bearing and rearing.

As soon as there was written history, therefore, there were records of attempts to prevent pregnancy. A four-thousand-year-old Egyptian papyrus mentions birth control. Greek philosophers discussed it twenty-four hundred years ago. When primitive and isolated tribes are discovered, they are found to have their own methods. The range of these, which are found in every corner of the globe, is astonishing—some with a degree of effectiveness, many more concocted of mixed myth and hope. Ingredients for contraceptives have included hearts of salamanders, camphor or quicksilver, honey containing the bodies of dead bees, froth from a camel's mouth, water once used to wash dead bodies. Diaphragms were made of grass, seaweed, dried figs, mustard seeds, beeswax, pieces of rock salt dipped in oil, pieces of sponge. Condoms were tried, made of bladders of goats, linen, animal gut, leather. An early version of the rhythm method was also recorded.[2]

The desire for effective means of birth control grew apace in the last century along with the desire to have healthier mothers and children, to relieve the economic pressures of modern society, and to support the push for education and upward mobility. Yet with the ineffective means available to people, the birthrate continued to be high, and the upward surge of population continued. In 1898, Sigmund Freud observed:

It cannot be denied that contraceptive measures become a necessity in married life at some time or other, and theoretically it would be one of the greatest triumphs of mankind, one of the tangible liberations from the bondage of nature to which we are subject, were it possible to raise the responsible act of procreation to the level of a voluntary and intentional act, and to free it from its entanglement with an indispensable satisfaction of a natural desire.[3]

As the West began to achieve more success with birth control methods and more political freedom to use them, the birthrate continued to drop. Developments elsewhere, however, brought the sharpest climb in human numbers yet seen. This came after World War II, when Western medicine, including antibiotics and vaccinations, insect and disease control, and other public health measures, were imported and applied in developing societies in a very short period of time. As a result, infant mortality dropped sharply and death rates in general plummeted. A decline in mortality that had taken a century or more to occur in Europe, now took place in a decade or less in some places.

In these largely rural and traditional societies, children were still seen as producers of wealth, not as economic liabilities. Old-age security depended on how many surviving children there were to care for the parents. The status of women in society often depended on the number of their children, particularly sons. An African saying held that "a woman without children is as the dead." For men, too, having many children was proof of maleness. Birthrates, therefore, remained at a high level. The gap between birthrates and death rates widened, causing population growth rates as high as 3.5 percent in some nations, which means a doubling of population in just twenty years.

Such growth rates are unparalleled in human history. Demographers calculated that in a hundred years, world population could be 30 billion people—though few actually believe the world could sustain such numbers. Concern over population growth was revived. Subsequent discussion brought general agreement on the seriousness of the situation but little consensus on what needed to be done.

The dilemma was noted by writer Dom Moraes, who was sent by the United Nations to survey the population scene before the World Population Conference. "The tragedy of the population problem," he said, "is that though every single individual born is desirable, people in the mass can be lethal without their wanting to be. By the time governments realize this, it may be too late."[4]

Churches, like states, found it difficult to shift their stance regarding fertility. Dr. Richard Fagley in a 1960 book, *The Population Explosion and Christian Responsibility,* spoke to the churches in words essentially relevant today: "A more adequate Christian witness in this area is a key to a more realistic approach by governments. Conversely, our neglect and inaction have been a major factor in governmental neglect and inaction. This is the point we need to ponder in penitence."[5]

As individuals and as a nation, we will be called upon to make difficult political decisions and ethical choices on population matters. We will want to find answers that preserve a profound belief in the preciousness of life and a commitment to a human quality of life for all people. To find such answers, we need first of all to be better informed of the dimensions of the population problem and of how it is interrelated with other world problems.

CHAPTER 2

Connections and Dimensions

If you have had all the children you intend to have, pause for a moment and see whether you can identify why you wanted two, or three, or six. Did you stop at two because you wanted to be free to do other things, or because of your age when you started having children? Did you have more than you originally planned because you kept trying to have a boy, or perhaps a girl? Did you have a large family (or a small one) because that was what your friends were doing? Do you think your parents influenced the size family you planned? Did your church? Did you ever do much conscious thinking about the subject at all?

If you haven't yet started a family, what do you think is the ideal number of children to have? Can you explain why you think as you do?

For most of us, it is difficult to pinpoint all the factors that have shaped our feelings regarding ideal family size. Our attitudes, motivations, and choices are apt to emerge from a tangled mass of hopes, fears, and myths surrounding matters of childbearing, which in turn are shaped by various cultural, religious, educational, and family forces. It seems fair to say that choices have rarely been determined by fears of a worldwide population explosion.

The young, black Ph.D. in Washington entering a challenging professional career will likely have ideas regarding ideal family size different from those of the young, white, farm wife of German Catholic origins living in Minnesota. The backpacker who finds it harder and harder to find truly wilderness areas in which to hike is greatly agitated thereby and may think there are already too many people. The laborer living in the teeming slums of Bombay, barely scraping out a living, will give not a thought to the worries of the wilderness buff but may find that the only real pleasures in his life center on his numerous progeny.

Just as the perceptions and circumstances of people differ, so do those of nations. Some nations with rapid population growth rates are already crowded and are confronted with the prospect that they cannot greatly increase their food production. Some nations with rapid growth rates have empty spaces that can become rich food-producing areas, with proper development. Some nations are small and resource poor. Some nations are small and resource poor but prosperous in trade and commerce and so are able to import enough food to feed their people. Some nations are unconcerned about population but are greatly distressed about the infant mortality rate and the high death rate of women from illegal abortion.

Brazil, bursting with vitality, long scoffed at the idea that its rapid population growth could be a hindrance to its development. More people, the leaders argued, create a push for innovation and greater production. They eagerly look forward to the day when Brazilians number 100 million and can claim to be one of the great and powerful nations of the world. Argentina, with a moderate birthrate, fears there will come a time when an exploding Brazilian population will need more food-producing lands and will look south to its less-populated neighbor. Argentina clamps down on distribution and use of contraceptives in order to increase its own population.

The Soviet Union asserts that population is never a problem in a Marxist system, tries to encourage the Great Russian segment of its population to have more babies so that they will not be eclipsed by other more prolific ethnic groups. China, claiming to be more purely Marxist, has the most massive and intensive program to curb fertility of any country in the world.

All of which is to emphasize that nations look at the population situation in terms of their own national background and goals, and define population policies in terms of their own internal needs, not in terms of some worldwide population explosion. Yet the cumulative impact is of worldwide dimensions and affects all nations.

The varying perceptions have created misunderstanding and tension. It was largely in the West that the new Malthusians began to speak of the terrible suffering that lay ahead unless ways could be found to slow and then stop population growth. Since they talked largely in terms of numbers alone, the implication seemed to be that the whole problem was the growing number of the poor. Developing nations, in reaction, pointed out that their populations were doing far less to exhaust natural resources than the smaller numbers of the rich. They noted that 17 percent of the world's population living in the richest countries were consuming 40 to 50 percent of the world's output each year. The United States wastes more energy than the poorest one-half of humanity uses.[1]

The developing nations, in various forums, insisted that colonialism and imperialism built up systems that kept them poverty-stricken and underdeveloped. Change the rules of trade and the international monetary system, they asked, so that we will have equitable opportunity for development. Then the population problem will take care of itself, just as the birthrates of the West declined as development proceeded.

18

CONNECTIONS AND DIMENSIONS

The developed nations, in turn, have asserted that poverty can never be eradicated while populations are growing so rapidly, that rapid population growth itself interferes with development, and that poverty must be attacked directly as a particular problem with its own aspects and solutions. Eventually, depletion of resources and degradation of the environment will adversely affect the quality of life for all—and even threaten world peace. However equitable the system, the earth can feed only so many people.

Essentially, there was truth in both positions, but for a long time neither side seemed to be listening to the other's point of view. Increasingly, the positions are intersecting, making effective and concerted action possible. Increasingly, too, there is more understanding that world problems do not exist in isolation and should not be placed in competition as to their ranking order. The hunger problem is related to the poverty problem and the unemployment problem, the resource problem is related to the inflation problem. All are interconnected, and the rapid growth of world population makes it more difficult to achieve progress in solving the others.

In a brief look at the world hunger situation, we can trace how some of these strands are interwoven. In looking at hunger and population, of course numbers are very important, but, beyond that, population distribution and population movements are also involved.

Constantly mounting population means a never-ending drive to increase food supplies every year, and, if nutritional levels are actually to improve, at a rate faster than the numbers of people increase. The good harvests of the mid seventies and the bumper U.S. crops dissipated some of the concern over the world food situation. Nonetheless, the medium- and long-range situation is still precarious. Despite the fact that grain production in recent years has grown more rapidly in the poor countries than in the developed countries, per capita production actually declined in these countries from 1960 to 1974 because of the more rapid rate of population growth.

A generation ago, the most urbanized region in the world—Western Europe—was the only grain-importing region. Today Asia, Africa, Latin America, Western and Eastern Europe, are all net grain importers. A growing number of nations of differing political systems and of states of development import over half of their grain supplies, among them Algeria, Belgium, Japan, Libya, Saudi Arabia, Senegal, Switzerland, and Venezuela.[2]

Lester Brown reminds us that cropland, however, is not the only element in the food supply. All life is dependent on four biological systems, the others being the ocean food chain, the grassland, and the forests. They are the foundations of the global economic system. Our growing numbers plus our growing aspirations are now exerting great pressures on these biological systems. Stress on these systems on a localized basis is nothing new; what is new is the speed and scale at which biological resources are being impaired and destroyed now. One effect is worldwide inflation. When offtake exceeds the regenerative capacities of the systems, the real costs of production can only rise, and the threat to humanity's future well-being increases.[3]

Population distribution is also a crucial factor in the difficult food situation. In many developing nations, the small farms are no longer able to feed and support large family units, since the land has been divided and subdivided over generations. Those without employment on the land head for the cities, along with many others hoping for a better life than the harsh struggle for a bare existence in the countryside. The growth of enormous urban complexes exacerbates the food problem because city dwellers are dependent on others to raise their food. Governments have to try to ensure adequate food for urban residents because unrest in the cities is much more politically explosive than misery among the more diffuse rural inhabitants. This results in the strange anomaly that the majority of hunger in the world today is in the rural food-producing areas, not the dependent cities. The rise of cities has closely paralleled the vast growth in food shipments from North America. It is estimated that forty years ago, about 5 million metric tons a year were shipped compared to an estimated 94 million tons of grain shipped in 1976.

Every aspect of the struggle to increase food production is also tied into the energy crisis. As the oil producers raised prices for their nonrenewable resource, the poorest nations suffered in their ability to buy needed fertilizers. Each urban dweller puts extra strain on energy supplies; for food processing, storage, transportation, and distribution are even more voracious consumers of energy than the production itself.

Hunger is a question of poverty. Those who cannot grow the food they consume must have money to purchase the goods they need. The flood of people to the cities and across national boundaries to other countries is caused in large part by poverty and a desperate search for jobs. The International Labor Organization estimates that at present, approximately 300 million people are unemployed or underemployed around the world.[4] There is a need not only for some kind of productive employment for these people but for the additional 1 billion who will be entering the employment markets of the Third World over the next twenty-five years. This enormous number of new job-seekers will result from the fact that around 40 percent of the population of the developing nations is under fifteen years of age. There are also several million unemployed and dependent persons in the developed world.

The United States too has found what an intractable

problem providing sufficient employment opportunities is. Part of our employment problem can be traced to a situation similar to that facing Third World nations. We too had a large migration to the cities of farm laborers, largely untrained and unskilled for the industrialized job market, forced from the countryside by growing mechanization. We also had our own baby boom after the Second World War. These babies are now entering the job market in a great surge. The number of jobs in this country has been growing continually, but the number of job-seekers has grown faster. Inflation—partly caused by the growing scarcity of natural resources and the greater expense of seeking new sources—has sent many women into the job market also.

Not only are people moving to cities in ever greater numbers, they are also moving across national boundaries in great waves. Again, the driving force for millions is the search for a better life. But whereas in the last century the millions of immigrants were leaving crowded Europe for the open lands of the Americas, Australia, or Africa, the flow is now going from the less developed to the more industrialized—and the goal is jobs. In Europe, the economic boom of the sixties drew workers from southern Europe and the Middle East, and they were welcome while the boom was on. They have become a cause of tension as they begin to complete with natives for jobs in a less robust economy.

The United States, across a long and little-guarded frontier, faces Mexico with one of the highest population growth rates in the world, some 3.5 percent a year, which means Mexican population will double in just twenty years. Mexico has had a stalwart economic growth rate for years but finds itself overwhelmed by the number of young people newly seeking employment each year—more in each successive year. Until recently, Mexico had insisted its population growth was not a problem and only in the last year or two has taken steps to institute a family-planning service. Meanwhile, untold numbers of illegal immigrants cross the border each year, perhaps as many as 1 million, and they are a growing cause of tension between the two nations and also within the political community of the United States.

Aside from the critical hunger issue, it is also possible to trace interrelationships of many other world problems with the size and rate of growth of population. The fact that such a large percentage of people in the developing world is children and young people, means an extremely high rate of expenditures for services for this dependent population. Large outlays for education and health services mean fewer resources available for capital formation to stimulate development and create jobs. Families are less able to accumulate the savings that would also fuel development.

The affluent United States remembers how it struggled to provide schools for the baby-boom children after the war. How much more difficult it is, then, for poor nations to provide for their much higher proportion of children.

In 1950 there were approximately 700 million illiterates in the world, about 44 percent of the adult population. In 1976, after tremendous effort and the commitment of massive resources to education, that percentage had been cut to 20. In absolute numbers, however, that means that today 800 million people are unable to develop their full potential because of illiteracy. Sadly, the number of illiterate women is growing at a faster rate, so that now they number two-thirds of the total number. In addition to the basic deprivation, the level of education of women also affects their fertility rate.

In the area of housing, the world has seen an incredible building boom almost everywhere, but still the makeshift shacks go up in greater numbers. The forests disappear in the search for fuel to cook the daily meals; fishing fleets of many nations compete fiercely for the thinning schools of fish; grazing lands become denuded and eroded and even become deserts, as too many animals are added to fragile ecological systems. The litany of world problems could go on and on, but the point is abundantly clear: Growing populations did not bring into being world hunger or poverty or bad housing or illiteracy. But the twentieth-century dream that humankind at last has the skills and the means to eradicate these ancient enemies, if only we had the will, is threatened by the sheer magnitude of the numbers of people who must be provided for—and the rapidly increasing numbers.

There are certain consequences that flow simply from the enormous numbers of humankind. To work on cleaning up one polluted river is quite different from having to clean up a thousand rivers—with many large cities on the banks and hundreds of large industries discharging effluents—especially when the rivers may flow across several states or even countries. The organization and control required to manage a city of 10 to 15 million are of an order different from running a city of 100,000. We are now working from such a large numerical base that small percentage growth rates have enormous consequences. A 1 percent growth rate in the Netherlands adds 170,000 to world population in a year, whereas the same rate would mean 2.17 million added in the United States and 9 million in China. A two-child average family in the United States would produce a population of about 271 million by the year 2000; a three-child average would produce a population of 322 million. It is important to remember that there is a lag time of about two generations after couples are merely replacing themselves before population would stop growing. For example, the U.S. population is still affected by the unusually large baby-boom generation born in the fifties. Only when that generation ends its childbearing and then passes from the scene, to be replaced by smaller generations, would our population growth cease.

As nations grow more populous and more interdependent, international problems become more complex and more urgent as destructive possibilities of modern weapon systems also increase. In *An Inquiry into the Human Prospect*,[5] Robert L. Heilbroner has given a dire warning: that under the unimaginable weight of the population now on the way, many nations may simply sink into a state of decay, despair, and apathy. Or—and this, he suggests, is more likely—revolutionary governments will arise that would have the will and determination to enforce, by whatever means, social reorganization and changes necessary to cope with the population flood. Such "iron" governments would carry other implications. They would be well aware that the developed world was living in conditions of infinitely greater wealth and comfort, which many in the developing nations claim were based on exploiting the resources of the poor. In a few years, even poor nations can have access to nuclear weapons, and that would open up the prospect of nuclear blackmail to enforce demands for a massive transfer of wealth to the poverty-stricken world. How would the rich world react? It is difficult to be sanguine in view of threats that were made during the oil embargo a few years ago that we might have to move in and ensure our oil supply by force.

Every improvement in the lives and economies of the poor nations in the future means increased competition for scarce resources. In the past, there was a belief that science and technology would always come up with the answers to take care of growing needs. A characteristic figure of this optimistic period is Buckminster Fuller, designer of the geodesic dome, who said in 1967: "Humanity's mastery of vast inanimate, inexhaustible energy sources and the accelerated doing more with less of sea, air and space technology has proved Malthus to be wrong. Comprehensive physical and economic success for humanity may now be accomplished in one-fourth of a century."

Such sweeping optimism is now much less evident. Each technological success has brought its own problems in its wake. Nuclear energy is now a source of much controversy and unease, and even its proponents no longer promise a new world of inexhaustible energy and unending growth based on it. Almost half of Fuller's quarter of a century has passed, and today there are many millions more who are unemployed, uneducated, sinking deeper into conditions of inhuman poverty than there were when he spoke.

Though hard, there may be some pluses in the realization that there are no simple, quick solutions to humankind's problems; that human commitment and intelligence and hard work are required; that no quick technological fix is going to do it all for us. Now serious planning is going forward on specific jobs to be tackled. The dialogue between the rich and the poor nations is frank and hard-hitting, laying out positions dealing with new political and power systems—not easy utopias. Not a lot in the world system has yet changed, but change is sure to come.

In the midst of this sober analysis of world problems, nations and institutions began to take seriously the problem of world population growth. How did this awareness begin to be translated into action? Let us look now at what is happening and how it all came about.

CHAPTER 3

Growing Awareness,
Growing Efforts

"Birth control is not our business. I cannot imagine anything more emphatically a subject that is not a proper political or governmental activity or function or responsibility." So spoke President Dwight Eisenhower at a press conference in 1959. Just ten years later, President Nixon issued the first presidential message on population. After discussing the world population picture and the need for family planning, the president stated that "this Administration does accept a clear responsibility to provide essential leadership." By that year, in fact, the U.S. government had become the principal source of funding for family-planning programs throughout the world.

What happened in just ten short years to cause such a fundamental reversal between the viewpoints of two conservative administrations? What changes had occurred in the political climate to make it feasible for a president to recommend funds for federal family-planning programs at home and for population assistance programs abroad?

The political climate was changing in response to acceleration of the process that had brought individuals and couples to decide that for various health and economic reasons they did not need or want as many children as families had had in the past. Although a major shift in social and political attitudes was taking place with astonishing speed here and in nations around the world, the changes did not come about without much heated controversy and intense political struggle.

The Struggle for Contraceptive Rights

At the personal level of this issue, the present generation of married couples is the first in history to be able to plan its families with a high degree of success. So commonplace has become the acceptance of contraceptives and the right to use them that we seldom pause to remember what a short time ago this right was secured—even in this country. The last state law restricting private use of contraception in the United States was struck down by the Supreme Court only in 1965 (*Griswold* v. *Connecticut*).

Something of the struggle can be gleaned from the writings of Dr. William J. Robinson, an early advocate of the right of doctors to prescribe birth control. In 1912, he spoke of the heartbreaking misery he saw around him every day because of the lack of knowledge or lack of means to prevent births. To a medical society, he said: "Our present laws regarding the imparting of information of the prevention of conception are in the highest degree brutal and infamous. . . . Introduced and dragged through by puritanical inquisitors, they are a blot on our country and a disgrace to our nation!"

He pointed out that the punishment for sending by mail any kind of information—even a suggestion—on how to prevent births was five years at hard labor plus a five-thousand-dollar fine. And there were "contemptible spies" whose job it was to try to induce physicians to break the law. "Remember," he said, "there is no cruelty like religious cruelty, and there is no brutality like the brutality of the hypocritical pharisaical puritan of the type of Anthony Comstock." [1]

Comstock was a morals crusader and special agent of the

New York Society for the Suppression of Vice, who became the symbol of those opposing any practice of birth control. Symbol of the other side, and best known of those fighting for the right to limit childbearing was Margaret Sanger. She made this her full-time cause after finding a woman, who had begged her for help with an unwanted pregnancy, dead from a self-inflicted abortion.

In 1916, she opened the first family-planning clinic in Brownsville, the most thickly populated district in Brooklyn. No doctor was willing to assist this effort; so she turned to her sister who was a nurse. All around the area they distributed flyers that asked: "Mothers! Can you afford to have a large family? Do you want any more children? If not, why do you have them?" Then followed details on the clinic.

They had no idea whether anyone would actually have the courage to show up, but on the morning the doors were to open, they found a line that stretched almost to the corner—at least one hundred people, women with babies in their arms, women with their young married daughters, a few men there to support their wives. All day and evening they came.

On the ninth day, the staff was arrested and the clinic closed. They were charged with breaking a law that said no one could give contraceptive information for any reason. Awaiting trial, Margaret's sister went on a hunger strike, and after several days a tube was thrust down her throat and she was fed by force—the first time such a thing had happened to a woman in the United States. This brought a great deal of publicity to the cause—and sympathy also.

The district attorney called women who had received advice at the clinic as prosecution witnesses. In rebuttal, the defense pointed out that there was a law that permitted doctors to give birth control information to men to protect them from disease. The lawyer then called back the patients and asked them how many children they had. The answers came: "Eight, sir, plus three that did not live." "Nine living, two dead." And on and on, the story of women living lives of exhaustion and anguish because of the law. Why should it not be legal to protect the health of women as well as of men? asked the defense.[2]

Sanger was convicted, and the conviction was affirmed on appeal, but the judge ruled that doctors could give birth control advice to married women for health reasons. Gradually, thereafter, the medical profession began to work more actively in this area, although the American Medical Association did not endorse birth control until 1937, and then only for therapeutic reasons.

Churches Begin to Change

Competing moral and religious values added intensity to the struggle for change in this area of life. For a period after the Reformation, Protestants and Catholics were united in their strictures against birth control. As Fagley points out, "Any other course seemed to indicate a want of confidence in God's providence." Eventually some church leaders began to sanction the idea that procreation was not the sole legitimate end of marriage, but this did not extend to acceptance of the idea of trying to limit childbearing. During the nineteenth century, however, there was a growing divergence of Catholic and Protestant opinion on this subject. Protestants, largely middle-class, were among those who began to want to practice birth control for reasons of maternal and child health and economic well-being. Since their pastors were married also, they were subject to the same desire.

The Lambeth Conference of the Anglican Communion had discussed the morality of birth control in 1908 and 1920 but continued to condemn it. The breakthrough came in

1933 when the bishops reversed their stand and somewhat ambivalently said that where there was a clearly felt moral obligation to limit or avoid parenthood, abstinence was the primary method, but if there were a "morally sound" reason, the conference agreed that other methods might be used "if done in the light of Christian principles."

The following year, a report was proposed that was to prove highly influential in the United States by stimulating public debate. Brought by the Committee on Marriage and Home of the Federal Council of Churches, the report held that while sex within marriage is primarily for procreation, it is also important "as an expression of mutual affection, without relation to procreation." Therefore, the majority of the committee held, "the careful and restrained use of contraceptives by married people is valid and moral."

The report was noteworthy also in moving from simply a discussion of limiting childbearing for personal reasons to a mention of overpopulation as a distant prospect that should be kept in view. During the fifties, major religious denominations moved to give their approval of the use of birth control.

Protestant rethinking on this issue brought about a new look at the biblical injunction to "be fruitful and multiply and replenish the earth." Just as planting too many fruit trees too close together on a plot of land will limit their fruitfulness, so, it was said, having a large number of children too close together is damaging to both mother and children. By extension, also, the fruitfulness of the earth—the preservation of God's good creation—depends on having the numbers of people in reasonable balance with the biological capacities of the world.

Pope Pius XII had declared at a 1954 conference on population that "the Church is not unaware of these problems; she is not indifferent to these anguishing aspects." The Catholic emphasis, however, continued to be on increasing resources to take care of growing numbers of people and insisted the answer lay in increasing economic development assistance to the poor, not in regulating the number of births to accommodate the public economy. And the condemnation of artificial means of birth control remained absolute.

A Politically Sensitive Issue

The fact that major religious groups differed so publicly and so vehemently on these questions made governments very hesitant to deal with them officially. Nevertheless, advocates of birth control continued to bring the subject up before the League of Nations and later the United Nations, not necessarily expecting action programs to result but thinking that any expression of approval by the international body would help to put pressure on governments to change their laws regarding contraception.

After the Second World War, private national family-planning movements began to emerge rapidly, and in 1952 these came together to form the International Planned Parenthood Federation. Some thought the federation was needed because of the threat of overpopulation; others wanted to stress the human welfare aspects of family planning, with emphasis on voluntary parenthood as a human right, irrespective of any economic, social, or political imperatives. The second point of view eventually emerged as the primary focus.[3]

Also in 1952 came the formation of the Population Council in the United States, through the initiative of John D. Rockefeller III. The work of the council initially was devoted chiefly to research, training, and technical conferences, but gradually its experts were drawn into a more activist role. Because much of the council's funds were provided by the Rockefeller and Ford foundations, another element of controversy was added to the growing population debate. The charge was that the rich simply wanted to control the poor by holding down their numbers. Despite this, the Ford and Rockefeller groups continued their work in the field. Other private groups began to set up family-planning services in less-developed countries as well as to provide population data.

Thus world opinion—and world activity—was nudged along in a variety of ways. The first venture in governmental international population assistance came in 1958 when Sweden gave monetary support to Sri Lanka to establish family-planning projects.

The first full-fledged United Nations General Assembly debate on population questions came in 1962, and it revolved around the question of the relevance of population growth to economic development. The specific issue was whether population assistance should be part of United Nations technical assistance programs. The answer still was no.

Nineteen sixty-three might be called a watershed year for international efforts. In that year, the Economic and Social Commission for Asia and the Far East (ESCAFE) sponsored an Asian Population Conference in New Delhi, accompanied by the usual flurry of opposition to the proposal for discussing "practical solutions to the population problem." The conference was attended by over two hundred participants from fourteen Asian countries and by five members of ESCAFE from outside the region.

The participants unanimously adopted a resolution that invited governments in the region "to take account of the urgency of adopting a positive population policy related to their individual needs and to the general needs of the region." Exchange of experience and information on population policies among member states was to be stepped up. The United Nations and the specialized agencies were urged to expand the scope of their technical assistance in this area.

A further step was taken in 1966 when United Nations Secretary U Thant accepted a declaration on population from twelve world leaders, stressing the right of individuals to determine the number and spacing of their children and to have the means to do so. This was reaffirmed as a basic human right by the 1968 Tehran International Conference on Human Rights.

All this laid the groundwork for the main thrust of United Nations program activity in the population field—the work of what was shortly to become the United Nations Fund for Population Activities, headed by Dr. Rafael Salas of the Philippines.

Salas felt that it was the intersection of two trends that finally made this international population work possible. One was the careful and analytical work of scholars in statistics, economics, demography, whose projections of future population size and future resource needs began to draw attention from politicians and planners alike. The other was the pioneering humanitarian work of private individuals and organizations that had initiated the work of birth control and family planning, largely from health and human-rights points of view.

The Debate in the United States

During these years of evolving activity on the international scene, culminating in the United Nations Fund for Population Activities, what was the United States government doing? For the most part, maintaining a very low profile! On many of the early votes in international meetings, the United States had abstained, largely out of concern for the large, vocal anti–birth-control constituency domestically. Eisenhower had spoken for many when he stated flatly that "birth control is not the business of our government."

In the late fifties it was the U.S. foreign aid mission that Ceylonese officials first approached for help with their family-planning program. They were referred to Sweden. To mobilize a change in U.S. policy would be too long and arduous a task, the Ceylonese were told, to be worth the small amount of help that might eventually be provided.[4]

Though contraception was now largely legal on the home scene, opposition retreated slowly. Typical was the situation in New York City, where there was an unwritten agreement that city hospitals would not prescribe contraception for indigent patients. Dr. Louis Hellman, head gynecologist in one of the hospitals, wanted to prescribe a diaphragm for a diabetic woman. Dr. Hellman decided to test the birth control ban and to do so in a way that would ensure widespread publicity. Planned Parenthood worked to line up near-unanimous religious and medical support from the non-Catholic community. The arguments were carefully defined to a wide segment of the public: Medical judgment in a life-threatening situation was being arbitrarily overruled; freedom of medical judgment, freedom of religion, freedom of information, even majority rule, were threatened. These arguments proved persuasive, and the incident ended with a victory for the birth control advocates and with a sense that political momentum was now on their side.[5]

The subject of U.S. involvement in world population matters hit the arena of political argument full force upon issuance of the so-called Draper report in 1959. The President's Committee to Study the United States Military Assistance Program had been created to look at the question of foreign-aid priorities and at whether too much was going to military assistance and not enough to economic assistance. It was composed of high establishment figures, including a number of military men. General William H. Draper, Jr., chairman of the committee, had a long-term interest in the population question based on his conviction that the sharp reduction in the Japanese birthrate had made possible the economic miracle in that island nation.

Committee members were reluctant to get into such a sensitive area but finally decided to include some vague language. There were no references to birth control but only recommendations for increased aid for maternal- and child-health services in recognition of the population problem and for research and information helpful to other countries in formulating practical population programs.

Even this mild population recommendation drew worldwide press attention as indication of a possible shift in U.S. policy. Eisenhower had submitted the report to Congress without recommendation, merely asking that they study it.

Concerned with what they saw as a dangerous trend, the U.S. Catholic bishops issued a statement in November 1959:

United States Catholics believe that the promotion of artificial birth control is a morally, humanly, psychologically and politically disastrous approach to the population problem. . . . They will not support any public assistance, either at home or abroad, to promote artificial birth prevention, abortion, or sterilization, whether through direct aid or by means of international organizations.

Once again, opposition actually helped to draw public attention to the issues involved, and with attention and discussion came greater understanding and acceptance. Organization after organization shifted to an endorsement of birth control. A number of groups sprang up to call attention to the population crisis.

All these factors made it possible for President Johnson to include a sentence on this subject in his State of the Union message: "I will seek new ways to use our knowledge to help deal with the explosion in world population and the growing scarcity in world resources."

Many actions were set in motion by that declaration. Lengthy congressional hearings followed, covering every aspect of the population situation. The Office of Economic Opportunity began to include family planning in its program areas. The Agency for International Development (AID) also began population assistance, though very cautiously at first. AID made it clear it would not consider requests for contraceptive devices themselves, only technical assistance and equipment such as vehicles and educational materials.

Only 2 million dollars were expended in that first year, but the amount grew rapidly to 185 million by 1979. Some of the funds go directly to other nations through bilateral arrangements, some is spent through private voluntary organizations working in this field, and a large sum goes to the work of the United Nations.

Official attention continued to grow apace. In 1969, President Nixon issued a full-fledged message on population, dealing with matters both domestic and international. He called for establishment of a Commission on Population Growth and the American Future; increased research to develop new birth control methods; a family-planning office in the Department of Health, Education and Welfare to provide leadership and funding for U.S. family-planning programs; high priority for personnel, research, and funding of population assistance in the Foreign Assistance Program; United Nations leadership with full U.S. cooperation, to meet the challenge of too-rapid world population growth.

The Commission on Population Growth and the

American Future was soon under way, headed by John D. Rockefeller III who had been interested in family-planning and population matters since his college days, and including a diverse group from various ethnic, religious, age, and geographic backgrounds. In its report the commission said:

In the brief history of this nation, we have always assumed that progress and the good life are connected with population growth. In fact, population growth has frequently been regarded as a measure of our progress. . . . Now there is hardly any social problem confronting this nation whose solution would be easier if our population were larger. . . . There is scarcely a facet of American life that is not involved with the rise and fall of our birth and death rates: the economy, environment, education, health, family life and sexual practices, urban and rural life, governmental effectiveness and political freedoms, religious norms, and secular life styles.

At some point in the future, the finite earth will not satisfactorily accommodate more human beings—nor will the United States. . . . How is a judgment to be made about when that point will be reached? Our answer is that now is the time to confront the question: "Why more people?" The answer, we believe, must be given in qualitative not quantitative terms.[6]

The commission came out with a long list of recommendations, including:

—provision of sex and population education in the schools
—measures to improve the status of women, including adequate child-care facilities and ratification of the equal rights amendment
—state statutes that would ensure access to contraceptive information, procedures and supplies for all persons including minors
—reform of state laws to make abortion legally available
—a high priority for fertility-control research

—national planning for a stabilized population
—sanctions on employers of illegal aliens

The controversial stance in favor of legal abortion at once drew heated opposition. Politicians were hesitant to deal with this issue; so in effect the entire report was quietly buried. Unfortunately, therefore, the American people were never engaged in considering as a whole package the basic questions posed by the commission. The questions are still to be dealt with.

Nevertheless, an enormous change in social attitudes and political acceptance had taken place in an incredibly short time. Similar struggles had taken place and were occurring in nations around the world in regard to the right of couples to limit their childbearing.

This change was exemplified by now ex-President Eisenhower who would say in 1968: "Once as President of the United States I thought and said that birth control was not the business of the Federal Government. The facts changed my mind. . . . I have come to believe that the population explosion is the world's most critical problem."

The dimensions of the problem were becoming clear. A growing consensus believed that action was unavoidable. What was not so clear—nor agreed upon—was just what kind of action needed to be taken.

CHAPTER 4

What's Happening Now?
What's Working?

On a busy intersection in Washington, D.C., heads crane upward to watch a digital clock on which numbers are constantly changing. This clock shows not the time passing rapidly by but the rapid growth in human numbers. Each five seconds 13 more people have been added to the earth's total. As the city's bustle passes by, grows still, rises again with morning's activity, the clock total moves inexorably upward—172 added each minute, over 10,000 each hour, over 200,000 in a day.

A sense that this momentum must be slowed became widespread in the sixties. But how does a world go about making the massive political, economic, social, and religious changes needed to lower fertility rates? In our day, sooner or later that calls for an international meeting, and in 1974 the United Nations scheduled a World Population Conference in Bucharest, Romania. While there had been earlier international conferences to discuss population questions, largely medical or demographic, this would be the first official political conference, where governments would come together to deal with public policy questions.

Once the nations assembled in Bucharest—135 of them—it quickly became clear that there were going to be major differences. The United States and some other developed nations hoped the conference would adopt specific goals for achieving cuts in birthrates by 1985. Third World nations were determined to press for consideration of broader developmental questions, claiming that the rich nations were using the population issue to avoid facing up to needed fundamental changes in international power structures.

This debate was aimed at scoring political points in world opinion. Few were arguing that development planning should not include family-planning and population programs. The other side was not claiming that cutting fertility rates would solve the world's poverty problem. The questions were more on emphasis than substance, but nonetheless the debate was exceedingly important. Because the language of the draft plan in some cases was weakened, many thought the conference a failure. Nevertheless, high-ranking delegates from many nations had seriously looked at the implications of population growth, distribution, and movement. And all the nations (with the Vatican abstaining) had agreed on a World Population Plan of Action, a signal achievement indeed. The basic thrust of the world's population agenda is set forth in the principles which declare: "Of all things in the world, people are the most precious. . . . The principal aim of social, economic and cultural development, of which population goals and policies are integral parts, is to improve levels of living and the quality of life of the people.

The Plan of Action then went on to set forth recommendations for action, covering such matters as reduction of infant and maternal mortality; assurance of the right of persons to determine the number and spacing of their children; full integration of women into the development process; promotion of education opportunities for young of both sexes; establishment of Social Security and old-age benefits; establishment of appropriate lower limit

41

for age of marriage. The sovereign right of each nation to decide on its own population policies, if any, was strongly affirmed. The plan also called for considerable expansion of international assistance in the population field.

Much discussion at the conference had centered on consumption by the rich as a problem for the world, an idea that the United States held was not a proper subject for discussion at a population conference. Nonetheless, action recommendation number 19 says: "Recognizing that per capita use of world resources is much higher in the developed than in the developing countries, the developed countries are urged to adopt appropriate policies in population, consumption and investment, bearing in mind the need for fundamental improvement in international equity."

Out of the developments that created the need for the conference, as well as being partly due to the impetus given at it, there has been a rapid movement around the world to set up national family-planning programs, usually in terms of maternal- and child-health goals. Looking at the world scene, almost all experts agree there has been a noticeable fall in the birthrate overall. The Population Council identifies declines in crude birthrates of 10 percent or more between 1965 and 1975 in 28 countries with a total population in 1975 of 3.05 billion. (All but 3 of these countries have received support from the U.S. Agency for International Development.) This represents a much faster decline than that which took place in the West.

Those facts represent the positive side of what is happening. Less reassuring are some other factors: Much of the estimate of world decline is based on the presumed fall in the birthrate in China, where hard figures are actually impossible to come by. Outside China, greatest success has been in small nations. Also, percentage falls of 10 or 15 percent in the birthrate can still mean that populations are growing very rapidly. As yet, very few nations have set or even considered population goals.

Development vs. Family Planning

In the absence of hard data, the debate, sometimes strident, has continued between what we may label for convenience the *developmentalists* and the *family planners*. The former base their case largely on the so-called demographic transition of the West. There the movement from a high birthrate/high death rate to a low birthrate/low death rate took place before there was any such thing as family-planning services. Only modernization and equitable social and economic development in today's poor countries would bring about the same result, developmentalists argue.

The other side argues that the ability to control fertility should be a basic human right and that family-planning services are crucial contributors to maternal and child health. To wait until social and economic development takes place before being concerned with fertility control is simply another form of the discredited "trickle-down theory," with women as the victims of the theory this time. Furthermore, additional research into the demographic transition reveals that the movement in fertility rates in the West was far from uniform and that in some cases they fell sharply in areas that were still poverty-stricken, rural, and traditionalist.

Neither with family-planning services nor with the developmental factors can exact correlations with a falling birthrate be proved. Nevertheless, there is growing evidence that certain socioeconomic variables do encourage lower fertility rates, among them education and

43

opportunities for broader participation outside the home for women; lower rates of infant mortality and higher age of marriage; movement toward basic economic security; modernization/industrialization for the society. It is also evident that where birthrates have fallen in recent years, family-planning programs are extensive or expanding. In other words, there is now enough knowledge, if not absolute certainty, to move into strong action programs.

Since each national program must be unique, much experimental work is going on. Some nations are inundating their villages and countryside with contraceptives; some are using peer pressure to change attitudes. Some are offering incentives; others are applying disincentives to discourage childbearing. Often programs involve the use of paraprofessional medical personnel—women reaching out to other women. In others, the most modern media motivational approaches are applied. Most programs are a combination of these ingredients and more.

One of the most rapid declines in fertility took place in Japan after the Second World War. In the confusion and turmoil of the evacuation from China, a "genetic purity" program was started, which allowed women to have abortions. Because other methods of birth control were illegal or unavailable, women flocked to doctors to have abortions, and the Japanese birthrate plummeted. This became the primary means of fertility control, and it is only now that the Japanese are beginning to try to encourage use of other methods.

Small nations with impressive achievements in lowering fertility are South Korea, Taiwan, Malaysia, Singapore, Hong Kong, Costa Rica, and Colombia. It is noteworthy that these represent a wide range of political and economic systems, cultures, and geographical locations.

Indonesia: An Important Success

In Indonesia, the world's fifth most populous nation composed of five major and thousands of smaller islands, the government of President Suharto ordered family planning to become a high priority, a reversal in policy from the pronatalism of the previous era. The government program started in 1969 and was in full swing in 1971. The United Nations–sponsored World Fertility Survey found in 1976 that in just five years the average rate of childbearing had dropped by over one-third in Bali, from 5.8 to 3.8 children, by 17 percent in both Central Java and Jakarta (Indonesia's capital), and by 15 percent in East Java. This success is all the more remarkable in the light of factors usually said to make acceptance of family planning very unlikely—a national per capita income of just $180 a year, an overall infant mortality rate close to 150 per 1,000 live births, 50 percent illiteracy among adult women, and a wide diversity of ethnic groups, cultures, languages, and religions.

According to a report by the Population Reference Bureau,[1] the heart of the Indonesian program is the clinics—often just a few hours a week in the local health center or a village official's home during which trained nurses and doctors are exclusively available for family-planning consultation. These are backed up by the field workers who travel their "territories," knocking on doors, telling people about the advantages of spacing pregnancies, and giving information on the clinic location and hours. In recent years, they have also begun to distribute contraceptives. The most successful field workers are those most like the people they are trying to motivate—married women of relatively little education.

There is a strong emphasis on centering the program in the village, which helps it to conform with the cultural,

45

ethnic, and religious patterns of each particular area. In Bali, for example, the program is run by the council of the strong *banjar* (hamlet), a traditional center in which all the families are represented.

A map of all houses is now displayed prominently in the banjar hall, with houses of IUD (intrauterine device) -users outlined in blue, pill-users in red, condom-users in green, and houses of noncontraceptors left blank. The contraceptive issue is discussed at each monthly meeting of household heads. If an apparently fertile couple are not trying for a pregnancy and are also not using contraceptives, the husband will be questioned.

In some areas of East Java, the village leader daily raps a signal on a hollow wooden instrument to remind the village women to take their pills.

Reaching the outlying islands of Indonesia will be much more difficult, and the program in general still has far to go. Up to now, nonetheless, the program overall has shown striking results and will be watched with great interest.

Mexico: A Long Way to Go

An even newer program that will be of particular interest to the United States is that in Mexico. Mexico, which now has one of the highest population growth rates in the world, long had a law that called for an increase in the birthrate and an increase in immigration into Mexico. "To civilize is to populate," proclaimed Luis Echeverria Alvarez while campaigning for the presidency. Barely two years later came the first official sign of change in this policy, as the secretary of the Ministry of Finance and Public Credit stated at an international conference that if present trends continued, "we will continue to see millions of children who either will die before reaching adolescence or, should they survive, will be unable to satisfy their minimum needs for education, health and employment." At that time, more than half of Mexico's children were born out of wedlock, and officials were aware of at least 400,000 illegal abortions a year.[2]

Echeverria's government thus initiated an official family-planning program, and it is now gathering momentum under the current administration. One of the features of the Mexican plan is a heavy emphasis on education. A curriculum will go into the schools at every level, not to separate the population subject from others but rather to permeate other subjects with that of population. The curriculum will cover sex education, self-awareness, world population and where Mexico fits in, the Mexican population and where the individual fits into that. There will also be a strong effort to reach young people through teen counseling and clinics.

A number of private outside agencies are being called in to assist, but the program is clearly the Mexican government's, and most observers think national leadership has a real commitment to making the program succeed. The immediate goal is to bring the growth rate down to 3 percent as soon as possible (a rate that still means a doubling time of about twenty-three years).

Is Religion a Constraint?

Are there religious constraints today acting as obstacles to the success of family-planning programs? Certainly there are religious beliefs and practices that if not acknowledged and respected can cause difficulties. For example, in Hindu Bali the IUD proved acceptable since there was no particular objection to a male doctor's inserting one. For Muslims it is unacceptable for a male to examine a woman, and therefore few women in Muslim areas would accept an

47

IUD. Where a smorgasbord of services offers a choice, religion need not defeat family-planning efforts.

In various developing countries with rapid growth rates, Catholic bishops have given their support for efforts to slow population growth. In 1972, in a message to the Mexican people, the Catholic bishops there held that civil and church authorities had a duty to prepare Mexican couples to make a conscious and responsible decision about the size of their families. "The decision which Mexican couples take as to the means, loyally following the dictates of their own conscience, should leave them at peace with themselves, and they should not feel that they have been cut off from the love of God."

Often, what seems religious opposition may more truly be labeled tradition and culture. Typical is an old Colombian saying that when a child is born "he comes with bread under his arm"—that is, God will see that the child is looked after. The attitude that children simply come and must be accepted is really changed only by modernizing situations that open minds to new ideas rather than by challenging anything truly a part of religious beliefs. Sometimes it is true also that political leaders will use religion as a cover for their own political goals—or for their desire to maintain their traditional preserves of power.

The fact is that churches have long been quietly and deeply involved in assisting in the family-planning movement as a health concern, as a factor in improving quality of life, and as a liberating force in the lives of people. As one medical missionary said, "To hold the trust of the people, we must be absolutely as concerned with infertility as with helping those who want to limit their childbearing."

Around the world there are many examples of creative individual mission programs having an impact in this area. One such is in the country of Zaire. There, a United Methodist missionary, Louise Gilbert, works in the remotest villages to establish dispensaries and clinics and to train workers do family planning. At the national level, Esther and Ralph Galloway, a United Presbyterian couple, work in the same field for the Church of Christ in Zaire.

They work closely with the president of the unified Protestant church, Dr. Bokealele, who feels strongly that family planning is an important part of the mission of the church. The program has moved deliberately, according to the understanding and desires of the people. In the parishes, groups want to give very serious thought to the morality of limiting births. Does it interfere with God's will? Is it destroying life? With church leadership, they work through their own theological understanding of childbearing.

The relationships of men and women also have to be worked through. In the past, after the birth of a baby, there was "separation of bed" or "separation of body," which meant abstinence for the woman and liberty for the man. Now, says Esther Galloway, the women are changing too. They no longer want to accept "separate mattresses." They say, "We love our husbands and want them by us," and the men are listening.

For most people in Zaire, the desire is still for large families. Accepting the idea of planned spacing and some degree of limitation is the first big step. Once that is taken, a rapid decline to a small family norm could take place quite swiftly.

A highly unusual church-related program is carried on in the Philippines by the Iglesia Ni Christo, a unique religious organization founded in the Philippines in 1914. Their work started with a pilot project that was to run six months and was aimed at gaining five thousand new "acceptors" for family-planning practices. Within the six months, the project recruited sixty-nine hundred and became nation-wide, with twelve mobile clinic teams and twelve follow-up units deployed over the country. Its most unusual feature, perhaps, is the close involvement of the church structure in the vigorous promotion of family planning. Some critics claim that the promotion is so vigorous that it sometimes becomes coercive.

Ministers deliver series of sermons on family planning. The church's own radio network encourages family planning, as does the official monthly publication. When the mobile clinic teams are coming to a parish, the schedule is announced in worship services. Teams promote family planning door to door and leave supplies of pills and condoms with local Iglesia Ni Cristo churches. Volunteer workers who are lay officials of the church, deaconesses and deacons, officers and members of the youth and married couples' groups, seek to motivate eligible couples, report complaints, assist in follow-up, and provide contraceptive supplies.

Churches Work Around the World

In 1965 Church World Service, the cooperative assistance agency of the National Council of Churches, began a Planned Parenthood Program. In that first year, with a budget of only $15,000, over 200 church-related doctors in 39 countries were supplied with information and contraceptive supplies. Gradually the program grew, and by 1968 had contacts in 81 countries. Since that time, the agency has moved far beyond the mere provision of contraceptive supplies into funding innovative projects in many lands, often in remote areas, sometimes in countries where government funding would not have been welcome.

In 1977, the program name was changed to the Family Life and Population Program of Church World Service. The feeling was that the term *planned parenthood* evoked a restrictive image of a simple birth control and contraceptive ideology, and Church World Service wanted to emphasize that the basic purpose of the program is to enhance the full development of individuals in both their community life and their family life. Among the listed criteria for selecting programs for funding are:

—that a project proposal originate from a community/country in the Third World;
—that its general program objectives are "felt needs" of the community, closely related to social, cultural, and economic needs;
—that it is coordinated with other related programs in community development, i.e., agricultural extension programs, health, nutrition, and so forth;
—that the project is voluntary in nature and that it offers a wide range of population/family life/family-planning educational, information, and clinical services;
—that the project has access to areas that are not currently reachable by government programs or areas where no government program exists;
—that the project is an opportunity for Christian witness, having a spiritual impact for bettering human lives far beyond physical, social, and mental well-being.

Examples of projects cover a wide range: motorcycles for the female coordinators in the Dominican Republic; a moderator for a conference in Bangladesh to begin to define a role for Muslim religious leaders in family-planning programs; salary for a consultant to help organize a family-planning and health project with the Nepal Women's Organization; financing to help start a newsletter aimed at young people in Manila to carry frank, straight talk on responsible family life; money for an outboard motor and a canoe to carry family-planning supplies and educational materials to the different Solomon Islands. Of course, more traditional clinical assistance is also supplied.

Director Lumen Rodriguez believes the church involvement can make unique contributions because it does not have to go through so many layers and channels and hierarchies as many other private organizations and government agencies do but can relate directly to people, face-to-face with those who will get the funding. "We can see the impact on their lives directly," she says.

Many of the Church World Service projects are done in conjunction with Family Planning International Assistance (FPIA), established in 1971 by the Planned Parenthood Federation of America. FPIA receives money from the Agency for International Development to distribute medical and other equipment, contraceptive supplies, and information and educational materials. Through full-time, multidisciplinary teams of family-planning specialists, it can provide on-the-spot expertise as requested.

FPIA often works through church-related institutions abroad. Like the Church World Service program, it seeks indigenous groups to work with which might not be possible for offiicial governmental agencies. As one example, the agency sent out a mailing to three thousand small social service agencies in Bangladesh in their own language, asking if they might be interested in doing something in family planning. They got responses from about five hundred agencies, some of them very small. No one had previously been in touch with them; yet they serve many of the poorest people in need.

Much is going on around the world, with governments, private organizations, and churches working in a myriad of ways. There have been many disappointments but successes also. Yet much of what happens to the world in moving toward population stabilization depends on two nations only—China and India. They also are moving strongly in this field but in very different fashion. Let us turn now to examine what is happening in the two giants.

CHAPTER 5

More Than One-Third of the World's People

Almost one out of four people in the world is a citizen of the People's Republic of China. Nearly one out of every six is a citizen of India. The fact that these two vast nations together contain one-third of the people of the world and that they are continuing to add additional millions each year is of importance to all humanity. Your life and mine, the lives of all of us, will be profoundly affected by the success or failure of their efforts to slow down and eventually stop their population growth.

Just one example: China has been seeking to raise all of its people from the brutal poverty that has been their lot for so long. China is modernizing and industrializing at a steady rate and is attempting to step up the pace. Until recently, they had tried to be self-reliant and self-sufficient and insofar as possible had depended on their own labor and resources. Now, as the needs of the Chinese are growing, they are moving more and more onto the world scene. As China achieves its goals for modernization and for a higher standard of living for its nearly one billion people, that means added competition for key but diminishing resources.

Both China and India have long known that to achieve their goals for their nations and their peoples, they will have to control population growth. Because of the impact of these two giants, we need to be aware of their efforts.

How have they gone about it? How successful are their policies?

The First National Population Policy

India was the first nation to enunciate an official population policy. The first Five-Year Plan after independence, covering the years 1951–1956, recognized the need to stabilize population to balance the resources of the nation with the numbers of its people.

In India as late as 1921, epidemics, famine, and chronic malnutrition killed nearly as many people each year as were born. (The birthrate was 48.1 per 1,000 people; the death rate was 47.2 per 1,000.) Then better health services and other modernizing trends began to cut the death rate, and by 1931 the birthrate was exceeding the death rate by some 10 points per 1,000. As the death rate continued to fall, the gap continued to widen, and the population to grow more rapidly. In the decade of the sixties, population grew nearly 25 percent, adding 108 million people to the total, the largest number for any decade so far. For, although the birthrate was now falling, the percentage of growth was added to a steadily increasing base.

In response to this, successive five-year plans placed increasing emphasis on lessening population growth by means of providing contraceptive services and improved social and economic conditions.

And the result of all the plans? In 1978, the birthrate had fallen to about 34 per 1,000, while the death rate had fallen to 14. Thus India still is growing at a rate that would double the population in about thirty-five years. Forty percent of the Indian population is under fifteen years of age, which holds the possibility of an even greater upsurge in the birthrate for the future. As of 1976, it was estimated that only about 15 percent of married Indian women used modern contraceptives.

When one looks at the social, political, and economic problems facing India, it is not hard to understand the difficulties of making sweeping social changes occur quickly. India is a land of some 560,000 villages, where most of the people still live. There are hundreds of languages and ethnic groups; there are sharp religious and caste differences. Most of the people are poor; many live in conditions of desperate poverty. Most of the people are illiterate; 80 percent of the women are. They struggle with chronic ill health; 1 out of 1,000 will die of tuberculosis alone each year. Their daily lives are defined by ancient traditions—the hardest, as someone has said, of all windmills to tilt at.

In the Hindu society, the woman is brought up to expect to have babies as soon as she is mature. Typically, she moves from dependency on her father to her husband and to her son if she is widowed. For the vast majority, this system furnishes their only protection, and within it the bearing of children furnishes virtually their only status.

Perhaps because the need and the problem were so great and resources so limited, the population planners seemed to yearn for a simple means of expediting matters. Thus in the sixties, there was a widespread belief that the IUD was surely the contraceptive answer for India. A doctor could insert it and move on; it did not depend on the woman's being able to read and understand directions; it did not create problems of privacy or storage space. But, unfortunately, it did create medical complications for some women, and reports of this spread quickly by word of mouth. As a consequence, the IUD became highly unpopular, a severe blow to a struggling program that did not need any additional problems.

Various gimmicks and approaches have been tried.

There has been an attempt to saturate the villages with condoms, using small entrepreneurs who would make a tiny profit, in the hope that the profit motive would help to push the product. There were mass vasectomy camps with various kinds of incentives offered to the patient—and to the person who brought him in.

Dom Moraes describes another gimmick: an attempt to push the rhythm method. Women who wanted to participate were given colored beads: green beads to mark the dangerous days, red beads for the safe days. The beads, however, had no attraction as ornaments; so they were given to children as playthings. The children would, of course, shift the beads around, making them meaningless as counting devices. Fifty percent of the women using them became pregnant.[1]

In all this, what has not existed is a full range of easily available fertility services, making choice a reality for all.

In the best-known public relations effort, India was flooded with the symbol of a happy family, showing parents with two or three children. The symbol became familiar to almost everyone. But that did not mean it became relevant to the lives of people who knew they would not be richer if they had only two children—and indeed might very well be poorer without the extra hands to work.

India Steps Up Its Efforts

At the World Population Conference in Bucharest, India was among those asserting that development was the best contraceptive. As India's troubles multiplied, however, officials began to think of more rigorous direct measures to slow population growth. Dr. Karan Singh, minister of health and family planning under Indira Gandhi, stated that while the real enemy was poverty, there was simply not time to wait for education and economic development to bring about a drop in the birthrate. Monetary incentives to individuals and groups were stepped up, housing and travel restrictions on the number of children civil servants could have were instituted so they would become models for the rest of the people.

The central government also agreed that if a state government decided to move to compulsory sterilization, it had the power to do so. "Our advice to the state in such cases," said Dr. Singh, "will be to bring in the limitation after three children and to make it uniformly applicable to all Indian citizens who are residents in that State without distinction of caste, creed, or community."[2]

While official compulsory sterilization was never actually instituted, the vasectomy campaign became more coercive. Quotas were set, and many civil servants were threatened with the loss of their jobs unless they produced a certain number of candidates for sterilization. As anger against the Gandhi government and its emergency measures mounted, the passionate core of the opposition centered on the sterilization program, and much of the blame for the government's fall was ascribed to this issue.

The writer was in India a few months after the defeat of the Congress party. Talking to various population professionals, there seemed little consensus on what effect this debacle would have on India's attempt to slow the growth rate. Some felt the effect would be slight and temporary, that now many people believe they have been castrated and when they find this is not true, the fear will wear away. Others say that all family-planning programs have suffered, not just sterilization, and that the effort is almost halted. One woman said the result has not been fear but indifference, that if you bring up family planning at a meeting or social gathering, people will say "Oh, that's all finished."

None of the professionals I talked to denied that there had been excesses, but they differed as to the extent and long-term effect of the excesses. In talking to average people whom I met as I moved around, however, I was shaken by the vehemence with which they responded to questions about the family-planning campaign under the Gandhis. The people told of pressures put on teachers and others to produce—by whatever means—a certain quota of men to be sterilized. Whether or not all these reports are true, the speakers believed them to be so. It was hard not to conclude that the cause of family planning had indeed suffered a grievous wound.

The administration succeeding Mrs. Gandhi's insisted it too was committed to the importance of cutting population growth. Shortly after taking office, however, Prime Minister Desai was quoted as saying that he would urge people to consider abstinence and yoga as means of limiting births. Desai said they would emphasize helping people to understand the benefits to their own lives of having fewer children.

Where, then, does India go from here? For two decades the central government and the state governments have been working to bring down the fertility rate. In many areas, India has made some remarkable strides since independence. The country increased its production of food grains approximately 2.8 percent per year from 1950 to the present, a rate significantly higher than the population growth for the same period. The result was a modest improvement in diet for many. The wide disparaties in income, however, mean the very poor still cannot afford an adequate diet. In the face of such poverty and the fact that social and economic change have not been enough to undermine the relevance of old tradition, the Indian villager, as one district doctor put it, continues to store up children like a squirrel storing up nuts for winter.

The Indian experience has been marked by erratic shifts, by attempts to find a quick technological fix, by a too-heavy concentration on family-planning services not integrated into other aspects of social development. Still, the birthrate has come down, and much has been learned. The future of Indian efforts in the population field, however, seems very unclear.

The Chinese Approach

While the population efforts of India seemed to be pausing at a crossroads, China was being hailed as the first major success story in terms of controlling fertility in a large, poor, developing nation. Still, while thousands of words have been written about the Chinese effort, we can actually be sure of very little of what is going on inside China. Demographic estimates by outsiders of the Chinese population vary by many millions, with the Population Reference Bureau estimating the population to be 930 million in 1978.

There is general agreement on some points: The Chinese population is huge and still growing; the Chinese government is pushing the most massive program the world has ever seen to end population growth, and the program is an integral part of the total development effort; the program is having success in lowering birthrates, but the degree of success is uncertain.

After 1949, the new Chinese leadership faced a huge and growing population and also the orthodox Marxist ideology that population can only be a problem for capitalistic countries where the people are denied the benefits of economic development. Nevertheless, as early as 1957, Chairman Mao, while proclaiming that "people are of all things the most precious," spoke of the need to keep population stable and in balance with food and educational needs. The Chinese program is not motivated by individual rights or freedom of choice but is one more element to be factored into the total plan to build the new socialist society. China's integrated development program includes literacy, basic health care, and employment for all; and a tremendous emphasis on raising the status of women.

During the Great Leap Forward, the Cultural Revolution, and the machinations of the Gang of Four (political radicals headed by Mao's widow), the "limited birth planning program" received less attention but has assumed a top priority in the greater pragmatism of recent years. It is typical of other mass campaigns at which China has been so successful and involves every segment of Chinese society.

The author went to China in late 1977 as part of the first American birth-planning group to visit China. We were a people-to-people group, not an official delegation. Each American touring group sees only a very small part of China, but the accumulation of notes and observations of many groups bears out the claims of the Chinese in regard to the health-care system. Through the so-called barefoot doctors and the mid-level health professionals, directed by fully qualified physicians, health services seek to reach every commune, lane, and factory. In our own experience, the first level of that care in a rural factory might be dispensed from a small, bare room with a shabby wooden table, a threadbare curtain hiding the examining area, a chair or two. Nonetheless, the *care* was there, nearby all the workers and available also to their dependents for small fees. Facilities were clean and equipment was sterile, and the personnel seemed warm and cheerful.

And always, our questioning revealed, the birth-planning work was going on. In every factory workshop or in every work brigade on the commune, there was a person responsible for family planning. Selecting a workshop at random in a lacquerware factory, we asked the guide to direct us to the responsible person. Immediately she took us to a young woman who opened a drawer at her work station, and there were condoms and two kinds of pills ready to be dispensed as people needed new supplies.

The clinics keep records on menstrual periods and contraceptive use for all the women, for these formerly private matters are now considered matters of legitimate concern to the whole community. When a young couple gets married (but not before; Chinese officials insist there is virtually no premarital sex in China), they are immediately visited by a responsible person, who describes all contraceptive means to them, and the couple can choose which they prefer to use. They will be expected to have their first child within a year or two, and then wait for four or five years to have their second, and preferably their last, child. All family-planning services are free, including abortion and sterilization. Should a young woman get pregnant "out of turn," she may be encouraged to have an abortion. Should she get pregnant twice claiming contraceptive failure, she would be lectured sternly about her carelessness, and there would likely be a suggestion that she be sterilized. That procedure is recommended to all after the ideal family size is reached.

The Propaganda Campaign

In spite of the stress on family-planning services, we were told over and over that, according to Mao, solving the population problem is not a matter of technology but of "ideological and political work among the masses." The new China was faced with the same problem as were other developing nations where the majority of people are rural and highly traditional in their outlook. There were no particular religious obstacles, but the deeply entrenched philosophy of Confucius was a tremendous barrier to change. Confucianism taught that men are superior to women, and therefore a woman's status was dependent on how many sons she could produce. One morning in China we met with a group from the Women's Federation of Nanking and asked them about life for women in old China. The old society, they said, was a hell in the human universe. Women were beasts of burden, and their husbands had the right by law to do anything with them. Sometimes, we were told, they did not even have names. Many women would have liked to stop their continual childbearing but did not know how and received no support from husbands or society. Sometimes they died from attempts to prevent conception.

Upon becoming the leader of China, Mao from the first made plain his intention that women were to be equal to men, and this idea is stressed continually to the whole Chinese people. In posters, plays, operas, women are always shown in productive capacities, even in heroic roles, with none of the sexual innuendos common to our country. Propaganda is aimed at women's accepting new responsibilities as well as at men's accepting new roles for women. Women are told that they cannot become educated and assume equal roles in building the new society if they have too many children; so they can see the personal benefits of limiting family size.

Dealing with these traditional attitudes was once expressed in a Chinese publication as the three-breaking down and three-establishing campaign:

First, break down the outdated idea of "attaching greater importance to sons than daughters and having both sons and daughters" and establish the new idea that "times have changed, and today men and women are equal." Second, break down the old concept that "one will have more support and help if one has more sons and daughters" and establish the new idea that "fewer children means better upbringing, and one should rely on the socialist collective economy." Third, break down the old concept that "giving birth to and fostering sons and daughters is a private matter of minor importance" and establish the new idea that "family planning is something of major importance to socialist revolution and construction."[3]

A story I was told illustrates how this would work in practice. A young woman in a commune that raised fragrant blossoms for tea had had two daughters and wanted to be sterilized. Her mother-in-law was very much opposed, and wanted her to keep trying to have a son. Women of the commune's family-planning association and of the women's federation visited the older woman and reminded her of how things had been in old China. She herself, they pointed out, had had eight children, five of whom had died in infancy. In the old days, women had not even been allowed to irrigate tea flowers; so lowly and contemptible were women that it was believed their touch might blight the tea blossoms. Now Mao had said that men and women are equal, and indeed her daughter had received some education and was able to work and participate fully in the life of the commune. She might even rise to be a leader, if she did not have too many children. After several such visits from her peers, the old woman was convinced and was happy for her daughter-in-law to be sterilized.

As this account—demonstrating the importance of helping the older generation understand new ways—shows, the new China is strongly based on the familial and communal ties of the old China. One is everywhere aware, in particular, of the care and attention lavished on the upbringing of the new generation. Children are beautiful, healthy looking, obviously the object of constant, loving attention. The fact that the two or three offspring are going to be healthy and educated also gives strong support to the campaign for smaller families.

It is clear that the newly liberated women feel they have

more at stake than do the men in this campaign, because apparently all the family-planning committees are composed of women. In the communes, factories, and housing projects the women counsel men as well as women, and they show their propaganda films and hold discussions with mixed groups. Still, it is women very definitely who assume the leadership. Another indication of the importance women put on controlling family size is that as rapidly as the number of sterilizations is growing in China, the ratio is about seven women to each male being sterilized.

The pervasiveness of population propaganda and the constant peer pressure to reinforce the family-planning goals, the easy accessibility to full family-planning services in a context of basic health care, the linkage of all this to the upgrading of the status of women—these are the elements that most distinguish China's population effort.

An official of the national health ministry told the American birth-planning group that China's goal is to achieve a 1 percent growth rate. How soon do you expect to reach that? we asked, but he would not speculate. Another official spoke up, "As soon as possible." We were told that the cities of China are at or below that goal, but the vast rural areas are a much more difficult problem.

This means that China no less than India is in many ways a question mark, though their population programs have been quite different. We have noted that China's birth planning is tightly integrated with its other social and economic programs, whereas India's often seemed to stand alone. China has had a full range of options for a couple to use in limiting fertility, whereas in India that is seldom true. India has set the goal of improving the lives of women, but as yet that largely affects only a few women of the upper class. It is clear to even the short-term observer of China that there have been remarkable changes in the lives of

Chinese women, though they do not claim they have yet achieved equality with men.

Many of the programs in India have been addressed to the men—such as the vasectomy camps—while in China the women, who have more to gain, are taking the initiative in birth-planning programs. China has a more homogenous population to work with, the overwhelming majority being classified as one people, the Han (or Han Chinese). India has many peoples, many languages, many religions.

In India, policies and goals are set at the top, and people are little involved in planning or implementation, and benefits may not be clearly visible. In China, while the people are not free to make purely individualistic choices, once the policies have been set by the Party, the people are involved in deciding how best to implement the goals in their own areas. Leaders in China at every level are expected to set an example. In present-day India, the word coming from leaders is confusing, and the future shape and scope of the program is in doubt.

It is hard not to be very impressed with the Chinese program and to believe it will be successful. Yet a 1 percent growth rate—still a future goal—adds 9 million to China's population each year. Only 11 percent of China can be cultivated; China must feed four times the U.S. population on approximately the same land area. China will soon pass the 1 billion mark, still steadily growing, and could move toward 2 billion before stabilizing. Can China feed so many? Can China continue to upgrade the standard of living for so massive a population? Will China's efforts become more coercive as the numbers threaten the gains already made?

Equally serious are the questions regarding India. Can it, within the democratic framework of which it is so rightfully proud, manage to bring about the tremendous social and economic changes that seem necessary to bring health care, education, and employment to all its people—and thus humanely help bring down its birth and growth rates? Can they devise a birth-limitation program that will have measurable effect, in time to avoid great suffering and disaster?

We can only speculate on what the future holds for these two giants. Our speculation is not idle, for our lives and our future too will be deeply affected by what happens to one-third of the world's people.

CHAPTER 6

Adam and Eve—And Others

In the biblical account in which Adam and Eve are cast out of the ideal existence of the garden of Eden, Eve faced what her role as bearer of children was going to mean in the fallen state: "I will greatly multiply thy sorrow and thy conception; in sorrow thou shalt bring forth children." In motherhood, woman has found perhaps her greatest joy, as well as limitation, suffering, subjugation. Motherhood has been profusely hailed as an exalted state and simultaneously has been the rationale for picturing women as weak, dependent, limited in talent and possibilities, of secondary importance to the male.

For many Christians through the centuries, woman has continued to be seen as the cause of the fall into evil and so deserving of the lowly estate that was to be her lot. "You are the devil's gateway," proclaimed Tertullian. "How easily you destroyed man, the image of God. Because of the death which you brought upon us, even the Son of God had to die."

Similar attitudes prevail in other religions. According to Will Durant in *The Age of Faith:* "All in all, Talmudic law, like the Mohammedan, was Man-made law, and favored the male so strongly as to suggest, in the rabbis, a very terror of woman's power. Like the Christian fathers, they blamed her for extinguishing the "Soul of the World" through Eve's intelligent curiosity."[1]

In Christianity, celibacy and chastity came to be seen as the most virtuous modes of living, but for the majority of women who did marry, their status was heavily dependent on bearing children. In Judaism and Islam, voluntary celibacy is a major sin. In the Talmud, even desertion by the husband was no grounds for divorce, but it was recommended that a man divorce his wife if she were childless after ten years of marriage. Though Mohammed insisted that "all people are equal, as equal as the teeth of a comb," he could also say that "a piece of old matting lying in a corner is better than a barren wife."

In some ways, early Christianity helped strengthen the security of women and raised their dignity by making marriage an indissoluble sacrament instead of purely a legal contract. Though barrenness was still seen as a tragedy, it did not mean that a wife could be so easily put aside for another.

The development and acceptance of modern contraceptives brought profound changes in the ability of modern women to plan for wider roles, even as access to education and industrialized society began to change concepts of what the proper duties of women encompassed. As the women's movement was developing on its own, the world-population issue began to draw more scientific and sociological attention to motherhood than had been given for centuries. In fact, the symbol of overpopulation was often the pregnant female, not the impregnating male. The population problem—for men to solve, naturally—became: How are we to get women to turn off this overabundance of fertility? The individual woman, with her desires, her needs, her potentialities, remained to a large degree invisible in the population debate.

Out of increased population studies, the conviction grew that fertility could not be cut back sharply unless women had wider opportunities and some degree of meaning in their lives not dependent on their roles as wives and mothers. At the World Population Conference, the need to improve the status of women quickly became the bandwagon issue by which most delegations wanted to prove their sincere intent—evidence itself that a great social revolution was taking place.

The final plan recommended "the full integration of women into the development process, particularly by means of their participation in educational, social, economic and political opportunities." The population relationship was noted, "Improvement of the status of women in the family and society can contribute, where desired, to smaller family size, and the opportunity for women to plan births also improves their individual status."

The Invisible Work of Women

New official and scientific attention has served to reveal how little attention has been paid in the past to the lives of women and the contributions they have made to their societies and economies.

In the United States, for example, the hours of homemaking and volunteer work that serve basic needs of our society do not appear in the gross national product, often used as an indicator of our economic well-being. Yet expenditures occurred in fighting increased crime or pollution, disease or more traffic accidents, would all be listed in the gross national product and therefore would appear to push up our assets, even though quality of life might actually be declining.

In all the work being done on world hunger and in all the development efforts aimed at agriculture, few have recognized that women are 40 to 60 percent of the world's agricultural labor force and in many cases are the effective operators of the farms. At a 1978 national conference on women and the food situation, speaker after speaker pointed out the lack of data needed as a basis for work on women's roles in this sector. We simply do not know how much nonmarket food women produce—how many eggs and chickens, pigs, milk from goats, vegetables from the home plot—because it has never seemed important enough for scientific study.

One development expert has pointed out that a woman carrying water on her head is taken for granted, but when a pipe is built to carry water into the village, its construction and presence add to the economic product. That seems to lead to the conclusion that a pipe contributes more economically valuable labor when carrying water than a woman does.

Now studies are beginning to reveal the extent of the backbreaking toil which is the lot of many women. In one area of Africa it was found that women averaged four hours a day carrying water—about eight trips lasting one half hour each, carrying containers weighing forty pounds. Other studies have shown that not only is the woman's work day much longer than the man's, but her agricultural lifespan as well. She starts working in the fields at a younger age and continues for several years longer.

Virtually her only source of assistance for this endless labor is through her own childbearing. As early as possible, children take over some of the jobs of minding animals or foraging for wood, which can also take many hours as the forests recede from the village. In many cases, the mother runs the whole family as economic unit by herself, as the number of families headed by women constantly swells around the world. It is estimated that some 30 percent of the rural families in the Third World are headed by women. A 1969 census in Kenya alone revealed that about 525,000 households had women at the helm.

As modernization proceeds, some of the small trading activities of the woman are eroded, making her status even more dependent upon her childbearing as her visible contribution to the society. Since her work is so often of a nonpaid character, it does not open up wider horizons and choices for her as the paid work of the man may for him. Though literacy is one of the most powerful ways of opening up new possibilities and bringing about social change, education is first offered to boys. Women constitute almost two-thirds of the world's 800 million illiterate adults. Helen Callaway, an American anthropologist studying nonliterate societies, has concluded that economic development and the expansion of primary education have broadened the gap between men and women.[2]

Because the unpaid work done by women may be invisible to development planners, their projects may actually make life harder for women. For example, if a modern tractor were to come into an area to clear more land, that may mean simply a larger area on which the woman would perform her traditional tasks of hoeing and gleaning.

Most top-level discussions on how to improve the status of women still consist of men talking to men, and various schools of thought put forth their conclusions without any particular effort to seek or to understand women's needs, ideas, and opinions. It was asserted in population articles for years that people in poor nations would not accept family planning until economic development occurred—in the face of the 30 to 40 million illegal abortions that were taking place each year, largely by poor women who had no other way of controlling their fertility. In some nations, this was the leading cause of death for young women. In 1971, the World Health Organization said the pain and suffering and death of illegal abortion was the most serious pandemic the world faced; yet there was no concerted international outcry over this health crisis.

What Do Women Want?

On the part of many women, there is clearly more desire to limit their fertility than was previously thought. Perdita Huston was sent by the United Nations Fund for Population Activities (UNFPA) to survey attitudes toward childbearing in six developing countries. Over and over again, she heard women say that they want to have smaller families than their mothers had so that their children can be educated and have a chance for a better life.

And time after time, she heard these same women say that they could not change their practices—and limit the size of their family—until their men changed first, for with the men lay their only security.

What emerged was one long, loud plea for more control over their lives and over their dignity as human beings. With few exceptions, rural women of the developing world say they live under the total domination of their menfolk. Rarely do they have any decision-making autonomy. That, they say, would challenge the authority (for which read also virility) of their men. Sex roles, tradition and superstition prevent most women from having any control over their lives from childhood on. . . . And most women admitted, sadly, that the issue of family planning was one over which they had no control. To dare ask a husband if he would permit the use of a contraceptive is a frightening thought to most women.[3]

"If I didn't give him a child every year, he would get another wife." And, "I don't want to have all these children, but my husband wants more sons."

Another common thread heard was that men are afraid that if women are free of childbearing, they will go gadding about everywhere, just as men have been free to do. And there is also the fear that with contraception, women will not be faithful to their husbands as they have had to be in the past.

Ms. Huston taped the experiences of Rachida, a Sudanese student, who was circumcized when she was eight years old: "It took five people to hold me down. The neighbors and the family came. It is like a ceremony. There is no anaesthetic and people keep saying, 'Cut a bit more here, cut a bit more there.' It is a primitive practice and it is stupid after all." The purpose of the female circumcision is to diminish her pleasure in sexual relations, thus helping to ensure her faithfulness to her husband. Still, says Rachida, circumcision for any future daughters will depend upon their father. "If he wishes it, I will do it."[4] That may be an extreme case, but in all societies the concept of maleness, of virility, has been very much bound up in the woman's childbearing and her dependence on her husband produced by it.

The mother with small children was dependent on the man to take care of her and the children until they were well up in years. When pregnancy becomes more a choice than an unavoidable risk, the woman's total dependency on the male is lessened, and his dominance appears threatened. For both sexes, in all societies, this new reality brings wrenching experiences as people see the constructs of their perception of their own sex as well as the constructs of the other sex inevitably changing. For women, it requires acceptance of new responsibilities; for men, it strikes at their traditional dominance.

In looking at possibilities for encouraging change in fertility patterns, it is clearly as to deal with the attitudes of men as it is critical with the attitudes of women. One United Methodist mission expert, in speaking of controlling population growth, said: "Forget the women for a year; concentrate on the men. Now they are fearful of their pleasure and their immortality, both of which their children represent. They are fearful of their little bit of power, which may lie only in the family. Work with the men—the women are already eager for change."

What Machismo Does

Dom Moraes, in the survey done for the United Nations during World Population Year, found machismo a problem in virtually all societies. In the Philippines, he said, "it is obvious that in the minds of most Filipino men their personality, their pride, is tied up with an idea of their own virility." In a Latin American country, a woman sociologist told him angrily that machismo operates at every level.

We have to change men, to offer them new values. Now they have only machismo, pride in the penis. A man here may have three or four different women to prove that he is *machisto,* and have children by all of them. In some areas of this country, 65% of all children born are illegitimate. Our policy is to try and educate men to look at a woman as a human creature, not simply as a source of pleasure in bed and a cook and a maid.[5]

For women in some transitional societies who have no education and no skills with which to compete in the paid economic sector, having successive children by a series of men is a survival mechanism—to ensure some kind of support for themselves and their children.

The problem of male machismo is by no means confined to the poor and traditional nations. Witness the long, difficult struggle in the United States and elsewhere to persuade men to take rape seriously as a violent crime, and note the still frequent occasions of derisive comments directed at the victim by judge and attorneys. Read the various debates over the legal option of abortion, where there is the frequent implication that women, unless protected from themselves by the male legislatures, will just have "fun" and then seek abortions for their convenience.

Without changes in the attitudes of men as well as women, fertility rates may fall not because of improved status but because of increased burdens for women. In Russia and other Eastern European states, legal rights for women are promised, but not much has changed for them in personal relationships. The woman has the right—even the necessity—to work, but after those hours she must usually take major responsibility for housework and child care. She has one, or at most two, children simply because the burden on her is too great.

In contrast, we have noted that China is putting a strong effort into changing male attitudes toward women as well as putting effort into changing women's attitudes toward themselves. The major reason for the campaign against Confucianism is to counter its emphasis that men are superior to women. If a man maintains his traditional role, mistreats his wife, and expects her to do all the nurturing and housekeeping tasks even as she works full-time, he too will receive the full weight of peer pressure to change his ways. His wife may move out, while committees of Party members and fellow workers visit him, seeking to help him understand the error of his ways. When he admits the latter, his wife will almost always return.

Changing roles are evident in moving about China, not only in the jobs women perform with quiet confidence, but also in the frequent sight of men with small children, bicycling them to school, sitting wth them in clinic waiting lines, and so forth.

Even though it is increasingly clear that male attitudes and practices are so important in the effort to reduce fertility, attention to this still lags. When this subject was being discussed some time ago by the staff of UNFPA, it was clear that there were few successful models for programs that dealt with the male role in fertility practices as well as the female role.

Special Attention to Men

A few leaders and governments have recognized the need for special work in this area. The Family Planning Association of Hong Kong has for the last year or two been targeting males there for special attention. One of their imaginative series of posters shows two men talking with each other and carries the slogan: "While we must depend on our wives to give us children, we can depend on ourselves *not* to have any." Since half of all families in Hong Kong have television sets, many spots with this same slogan are carried on television. They use well-known figures to repeat the message, such as a jockey, a soccer player, or the like.

The association also has a continuing series called "Mr. Family Planning Campaign." In this, two well-known comic stars represent husbands willing to use contraceptives. The hope is that Mr. Birth Control and Mr. Vasectomy, as they are called, will become household names. The pair does brief comic spots, always ending with the message on male responsibility in family planning. These personalities also occasionally appear at crowded public places, such as bus terminals, handing out condoms to all men passing who appear to be over twenty-one. The message on the condom says, "Have fun but play it safe." The Hong Kong association also sponsors five male clinics that have male nurses and their own advertising campaign.

In the United States, because of the popularity of the pill for the last fifteen years, there has been little male involvement in contraceptive measures. Some think this has encouraged male irresponsibility in this area. Now, because of fears about the pill, women are turning more to methods that depend more on partner involvement or support. Yet there have been few places a man could turn for information or counseling. In 1976, a contraceptive clinic opened in San Francisco—the Men's Reproductive Health Clinic, perhaps the first of its kind in this nation. The clinic deals with questions about birth control in which men participate, the hazards of the pill and the IUD, changing male sex roles, male involvement in the birth of babies, and fathering.

Such organizations as the National Organization for Non-Parents and some local chapters of Planned Parenthood have campaigns aimed specifically at male teen-agers, stressing responsible use of sex. They carry such slogans as "Don't Kid Around" and "Be a Teen-Age Non-Parent."

New guidelines proposed by a task force of the staff of the United Nations Fund for Population Activities illustrate the growing sensitivity to mutual responsibility in fertility matters. Typical are such points as these:

—Studies should be undertaken of the traditional roles of men and women in parenthood to point toward the possibility of an increased sharing of household and nurturing functions between men and women.
—Counseling should stress that the family and community responsibility for contraception should not be left to women alone but should be shared by men and women.
—The pattern in many national family-planning programs is that men occupy most of the policy-making and other high-level positions and that women work as nurses/midwives and medical auxiliaries and health visitors. In order to change this pattern, men should where possible be hired also at the implementation level and women at the policy-making level.[6]

Christ Treated Women as Individuals

The record of Christianity is somewhat mixed in regard to women. The attitude of fear and condemnation that marked the utterances of many church leaders and theologians through the ages did much to abet the suppression of the talents and abilities of women. In that, they bore no resemblance to the attitude Christ himself displayed toward women, whom he always treated as persons as capable and as responsible as men for making moral judgments and choices. He did not hand the woman taken in adultery a list of rules for her life; he simply charged her to sin no more. In the story of Martha and Mary, he wanted women to hear his teachings and choose to live by the way of life he exemplified. Christ always treated women as individuals, not as people confined to narrow roles of wife and mother.

In that spirit, Christian mission schools have often been the opening wedge that first brings a possibility for educating women. In that sense, their influence has been incalculable. Today, church programs abroad often have a heavy emphasis on leadership training for women. In the United States, many churches and church groups have been leaders in the fight to pass an equal rights amendment.

Some claim that the movement for women's equality is just a movement of spoiled and affluent Western women. It takes little observation, however, to see that this is a current trend all over the world, though specific forms and goals may vary in different societies.

There are many obstacles to success, however, and one of the most intractible is the problem of massive unemployment around the world. More years of schooling can postpone the time at which women begin bearing children, but education also creates the desire on the part of many to take on nontraditional tasks. Broadened education and opportunities for women are seen as necessary ingredients in any successful and humane program to reduce population growth; yet they also put more strain on limited resources for development and seem to require an almost impossible level of job creation. How is this impasse to be resolved? Perhaps entirely new ways of looking at employment will be required to make work available to those who want paid employment: shorter workweeks, shared jobs, sabbaticals for all workers, public service requirements for people at each end of the age span.

In South Korea, part of the fall in the birthrate may be due to the harsh lives led by thousands of young women now toiling long hours in the new textile mills. This bears strong resemblance to similar conditions in the sweatshops of the industrializing United States. In our country today, rising inflation plus our emphasis on rising consumption as being necessary to the good life have been much of the reason for women's entering the labor market. In various ways, then, falling birthrates may be partly caused by the expense and difficulty of raising children—surely not the most desirable way of cutting the birthrate.

There is much to be done to put the emphasis on having small families, not because children are seen as expensive burdens and that life with them is too difficult, but because we must all live sensibly within the limits of our world. To that end, we must work to ensure that each child is born into a healthy environment, has opportunitities to develop its own potentialities, and is enabled to grow into a productive, valued person. In such a society, men and women would be free also to choose not to have children, but all would be a part of a community loving and supporting those children born.

All of this requires some profound rethinking of the roles of men and women and their relationships to each other and to children. Women need to understand themselves as persons first, not only with equal needs and desires but with equal responsibilities. Men need to examine their attitudes toward women, toward sexuality and parenthood and be willing to accept women in a new light.

The Preamble to the United Nations Declaration on the Elimination of Discrimination Against Women says:

Discrimination against women is incompatible with human dignity and with the welfare of the family and of society, prevents their participation, on equal terms with men, in the political, social, economic and cultural life of their countries and is an obstacle to the full development of the potentialities of women in the service of their countries and of humanity.

That may not sound like a population policy, but in fact efforts to bring women into full participation in the national and international community could indeed be the most effective population policy of all.

CHAPTER 7

Ethical Questions: The Answers Concern Us All

The ethical issue is not whether population will be restrained; it is whether people will restrain it through actions consistent with humanity's most profound moral sensibilities or through inhumane or catastrophic methods.

Thus Christian ethicist Roger Shinn poses the fundamental question in the population area.[1] There can be no question that the carrying capacity of the earth is not limitless—although we may not know for sure what the carrying capacity is (and we can assume that it will vary with time).

Preceding chapters have detailed some of the attempts by public and private agencies to bring down the birthrate and thus control population growth. Some success has been achieved; world population growth has slowed somewhat. The question we face today is whether current efforts are bringing results fast enough.

Some argue that people act in their own rational self-interest. They will therefore perceive the impact that high fertility rates have on their own welfare and will act to reduce their fertility sufficiently without outside intervention. Others believe that we must make more intensive but humane efforts to see that the population stabilizes as soon as possible. Otherwise, they fear, oppressive methods will be applied later as conditions deteriorate. Still another school of thought insists that we have already reached the point where only Draconian measures now can avoid horrendous catastrophe.

In the face of so many unknowable and unprovable factors, the task is to ensure that people and resources are in a reasonable balance at any given time and to achieve that balance by means that promote equity and protect human rights. Already it is clear that initiatives in this uncharted field raise complex ethical and moral questions and require difficult choices. It may seem these questions arise on matters far removed from our own lives here. With all the other problems that seem to besiege us in this modern age, do we really need to worry about population ethics too?

The answer should be yes, for these questions arise in dealing with an area that is, says Drew Christiansen, "central to our humanity because it provides us with personal continuity and because it is a source of regeneration and renewal. It affirms that the gift of life is good."[2] Furthermore, these ethical choices involve both the shape and degree of our involvement in population policies and programs abroad, and also important issues facing us here at home.

There have been those who argued that it was immoral for the United States to be involved in population programs in the developing nations at all. They feared Western concern actually grew from a desire to keep down the numbers of the poor and to retain our control of much of the world's wealth. Some of this criticism has lessened with the rapid growth of national family-planning and population programs and with the rising requests for assistance in this area coming from poor nations.

Loud criticism of U.S. actions today comes also from those who hold that we only make things worse for the world by offering help to nations that face imminent disaster because of overpopulation. This is sometimes called the *triage theory,* sometimes the *lifeboat ethic.*

One of the leading spokesmen for this point of view is Dr. Garrett Hardin. As he explains it, the world population situation evokes the image of people seeking to save themselves after the sinking of a ship. Some people are fortunate enough to have gotten themselves into a well-provisioned lifeboat. Others are in leaky boats, able, though barely, to stay afloat if not one more person comes aboard. Other people are swimming in the ocean, desperately trying to reach one of the lifeboats and climb aboard.

We are adrift in a moral sea. We know our boat has a limited carrying capacity, let's say 60 persons. Fifty of us are already in the boat and more than 100 are trying to get in. What do we do? We have several options: we may be tempted to try to live by the Christian ideal of being our brothers' keeper or by the Marxist ideal of "to each according to his needs." Since the needs of all in the water are the same, and since they can all be seen as our brothers, we should take them all into the boat, making a total of 150 in a boat designed for 60. The margin of safety is broken. The boat swamps, everyone drowns, complete justice, complete catastrophe.[3]

One group Hardin works with, the Environmental Fund, has carried on an extensive advertising campaign to make the following points: (1) World food production cannot keep pace with the galloping growth of population. (2) Family planning cannot and will not in the foreseeable future check this runaway growth. (3) It makes no difference whatsoever how much food the world produces if it produces people faster. (4) Our past generosity has encouraged a do-nothing policy in the governments of some developing nations. In sum the ad says, "When aid-dependent nations understand that there are limits to our food resources, there is hope that they will tackle their population policies in earnest."

Many Americans find these arguments persuasive. After all, it is true that what we can do to shape the world is limited, and we have already put strings of various sorts on assistance programs. For example, a loan for rural development may be predicated upon the local government taking steps toward land reform. There are stipulations under which aid can be denied to nations with a consistent record of human rights violations. Assistance efforts are to be concentrated in those countries that take positive steps to help themselves.

If population growth is truly seriously damaging all other developmental efforts, why should there not be a provision insisting on population goals and effective population programs before aid can be granted in other fields? Why should not Christians support this approach, since our desire is not to be just sentimentally humanitarian to ease our conscience but to assist effective development in the poor nations?

In population concerns, perhaps above all others, there are sensitivities in the very nature of our humanity that must be carefully respected. The smallest suggestion that the United States was imposing population restrictions on other nations would almost surely create a damaging backlash—not only against our country but perhaps against the programs designed to reduce population growth.

The fact is that already 92 percent of the population of less developed countries live under governments that approve government or private family-planning programs. Thirty-three of these 63 governments (representing 76 percent of the population in the developing world) specifically support family planning as a means to achieve lower birthrates and not merely as a health measure for women and children. Growing awareness and commitment is reflected in increased allocations to family-planning programs, between 1972 and 1975 up 67 percent in Bangladesh, 137 percent in Indonesia, 515 percent in Nepal, 577 percent in the Philippines. What is needed now is clearer understanding of the interrelated factors that lower fertility rates, more resources devoted to the total effort, and stronger commitment by leaders at every level. What is not needed is heavy-handed prodding by the United States which could interrupt progress already being made.

After all, we are not snug and isolated in a secure lifeboat. Defining the world situation as such gives us a false picture of a we/them issue: *They* are having too many babies, which threatens disaster to the world. Why is population growth such a problem for the world?

As we look at the list of predicted critical problems, our own contribution to them emerges clearly. At present, it is the rich who are gorging themselves on the world's resources far more than the more numerous poor. It is the industrialized nations that are pouring the chemical and industrial poisons into air and water—though all nations are contributing to various kinds of pollution. The sheer numbers of humankind do threaten to exceed food capacity unless growth is stopped, but at present there are many internal structures as well as flaws in the international economic system dominated by the West that cause people to be poor—and therefore hungry. Instability caused by burgeoning numbers of poor and unemployed people will threaten peace, but worldwide there may be more to fear from the competition of the affluent for dwindling resources. All nations are wasting precious resources on ever-increasing armaments.

We do indeed need to be concerned with solutions to the problem of population growth; but it is morally incumbent upon us to keep in mind that it is only one aspect of the challenge of world development we face today, and concentration upon it should never become a means of avoiding other aspects of that challenge.

Beyond this general framework in which we should place our population activities, specific ethical questions are arising. Who should control the shape and content of population programming—the donor of funds or the recipient of them? How do we weigh the tension between individual rights and the well-being of the total community? If individual rights must be restricted, what types, what degree of coercion is permissible?

Who Should Control Programming?

Mindful of newly strengthened national pride and sensitivities, donor governments and agencies have tried hard in recent years to avoid imposing their own ideas and standards on developing nations. Our own aid program states that "United States assistance should be administered in a collaborative style to support the development goals chosen by each country receiving assistance." If local control results in policies or use of materials that would be considered unsatisfactory, dangerous, or unethical here, can we be free of responsibility if our funds are involved?

As one example, many of the successful family-planning programs distribute the pill through nonmedical outreach personnel. They do not give physical exams to women, but they are trained to tell women about possible side effects. The theory is that more women are benefited by taking the pill and thus avoiding too frequent or too numerous pregnancies than are harmed by its possible ill effects. Are we helping to foster unfair double standards of care? Or are we learning to reach beyond our own physician-dominated health-care system to assist innovative approaches that better serve the needs of the majority of people?

Dr. Allan Rosenfeld, professor at the College of Physicians and Surgeons at Columbia University, tells of an experiment in Bangladesh that recruited local women and trained them to work in the operating room, first as scrub nurses, then as first assistants. Eventually, they were trained to do the surgical procedure known as "mini-lap"—a tubal ligation. In evaluating their performance, it was found that by all measures, including morbidity, the locally trained women did as well as or better than the physicians. And two of the first seven women so trained were illiterate!

Concludes Dr. Rosenfeld, "Ethical concerns about unsupervised contraceptive usage must be viewed in this context: when the choice in developing countries is between the best care and no care at all, most people are likely to get no care at all."[4]

Another example arises in the use of Depo Provera, which is largely banned in the United States as a dangerous drug but found very effective as a long-lasting contraceptive injection by some Third World governments. In this case, the practice seems to be that the indigenous government should be free to make a choice such as this. When it is a question of testing new drugs, however, that is quite a different matter. An official of Family Planning International Assistance says flatly that they will not be associated in any way with a program that involves drug experimentation on the local populace, even where the indigenous government has given permission and may be involved.

A staff member of The United Methodist World Division says that denomination pioneered and is deeply committed to giving aid to indigenous churches in the form of block grants. This freedom to decide on their own needs and priorities is seen as crucial to the development of strong local leadership and structures. Not only the resources provided but the trust that they will be used properly is a kind of support for the self-development of peoples.

Consent for Sterilization

U.S. aid monies cannot be used to pay for the performance of "involuntary sterilizations." Considerable controversy has arisen, both here and abroad, over just what is necessary to ensure the informed consent that makes the procedure voluntary.

In the United States, charges have been made that poor women—particularly Indian, Hispanic, and black women—have been coerced into sterilization, against their will and even without their knowledge. It is claimed that women in labor have been asked by doctors to give their consent to sterilization; that non–English-speaking women have not understood the irreversible nature of what is being done to them; that doctors in training have used poor women without their knowledge to practice this procedure; that poor women have been told they will lose welfare benefits unless they agree to be sterilized.

Government regulations to prevent abuses have been on the books, but studies such as one made by a Senate committee headed by former Senator James Abourezk into practices on Indian reservations found that some doctors and agencies were not observing the requirements for informed consent.

Now the government, through regulations put out by the Department of Health, Education and Welfare, has moved to strengthen its procedures. New regulations require a thirty-day waiting period between the decision and the actual sterilization procedure. The patient must be given a full and fair explanation of the procedure, its benefits and its risks, with particular stress on the fact that it is irreversible. The explanation must be in a language the patient speaks and in words she can fully understand. A counselor other than the doctor must be present during this explanation. The patient must be told that she cannot lose any welfare benefits if she refuses to have the operation. All of this information also must appear on the consent form she signs.

Although these apply only to public funded procedures, so strong has become the public outcry for stricter regulations in this area that it is likely that all doctors and hospitals will observe the waiting period and careful consent procedures.

The question of informed consent has proved difficult in the United States. What should be the requirements in poor, rural societies overseas where many may be illiterate? Is informed consent meaningful in such situations? One official of a family-planning agency told me of observing women who had crossed the border of Burma into Thailand, often having to bribe the border guards. They had come many miles, to a hospital—normally an institution they would shun because of its association with serious illness and death—in order to seek out the operation they had heard about that would mean they would have no more babies. They had not been stimulated by professional "motivators" in Burma—they had come simply as a result of word-of-mouth reports. "Is this not the most real and dramatic example of informed consent?" he asked. Dramatic and real it is, but it is not sufficient to serve as a general means of protecting women or men from zealous proponents.

In 1977, a political uproar erupted when an AID-supported project in Thailand was accused of sterilizing women of hills tribes without their knowledge at such a rate that the tribes were in danger of extinction within a generation. Investigators were immediately dispatched, and they found that while the rate of sterilization was indeed surprisingly high for an isolated and illiterate people, coercion was not the reason. Instead, it seemed, sterilization fitted into their life-styles better than continual use of contraceptives. They had the number of children they wanted, and then sought the permanent method of preventing children. Women on the average had four children before seeking the operation, and, with low infant mortality, the tribes actually still have a rapid growth rate and a doubling time of perhaps twenty years.

As far as consent was concerned, according to the AID report, not only had the women and their husbands given their consent but, because of tribal mores, consent also extended to the in-laws of the couples. Even the village head man had to agree!

The International Program of the Association for Voluntary Sterilization is one of the most active agencies in this field. In dealing with consent by illiterate patients, the program's guidelines call for verification of the informed consent by the physician, a medical assistant, the marks of the patient and of a witness of the same nationality and sex as the applicant (patient).

Sterilization has become the contraceptive phenomenon of the seventies. Voluntary surgical sterilization is now estimated to be the foremost means of fertility control in the world, passing abortion in that respect. By the end of 1975, according to AID estimates, 65 million couples in the world had chosen voluntary sterilization, as compared to 15 million couples only five years earlier.

Just a few years ago, coercion in regard to sterilization meant denial of this service to those who wanted it. In many places it was totally illegal; in others there were complicated stipulations that in essence denied it. Both these conditions still exist, even as the practice has grown with unanticipated rapidity where men and women can obtain it. So quickly has this change come about, that proper safeguards which are protective but do not result in denial of this choice are still being debated and worked out.

The National Council of Churches and some denominational agencies did much to draw public attention to problems in this area, pointing up the important role private groups can play in advocating safeguards and monitoring practices both here and abroad. Local groups can do the same in their own community practices. The importance of doing this is undeniable. As Drew Christiansen points out, "Procreation is so fundamental to human personhood that to tamper with it without consent is to deny that personhood."[5]

Incentives and Disincentives

Another area for ethical evaluation is the use of incentives and disincentives in fertility planning. A number of countries have experimented with various types of these, with varying degrees of success. For example, Indonesia tried monetary incentives to field workers, giving them a small sum for each new acceptor recruited. Largest amounts were given for those recruited to use the IUD. This program collapsed under the weight of trying to keep track of thousands of tiny payments and in the face of complaints from the women who received the device. As one woman said, "I got the IUD, I feel the pain, and she gets the payment!"

In Singapore, tax relief is granted only for the first three children, paid maternity leave only for two children. Families with only two children get priority in public housing. In Tunisia, family allowances are limited to four children.

These matters may seem highly technical and internal to other governments. But the U.S. government and churches may support programs that face such decisions. Certainly

91

incentives and disincentives offer some degree of coercion. When do they become impermissible infringements on individual human rights and assaults on human dignity? To offer a starving man food only on condition that he be sterilized is clearly unacceptable, for that leaves him no choice at all. To offer a woman payment for each period she does not become pregnant leaves her free to accept the payment or not, so long as the daily wage that supports her is not at stake. The housing and maternity leave disincentives are harsher but again leave some choice to the individual. Such disincentives are humane only where health and family-planning services are adequate and available to all. Each case requires careful weighing of the competing rights to determine when the state, in order to serve the good of the whole community, may place restrictions on the individual right to procreate.

A World Council of Churches paper issued in World Population Year suggests that if a government considers that some intervention is required, that government must:

1. demonstrate that continued unrestricted liberty poses a direct threat to human welfare; that the common good is threatened;
2. demonstrate that the proposed restrictions on freedom promise in the long run to maximize options of choice;
3. see that the restrictions on free choice fall upon all equally;
4. choose the program that entails least intervention.

The document points out:

The teachings of Jesus have often been given an unduly individualistic orientation by being abstracted from the biblical ethos as expressed in the prophets, which provided the background of His thinking. He frequently emphasized the personal dimension of moral responsibility; but He also accepted and affirmed the social dimension from the Old Testament heritage. Thus the Christian concern focuses both on the family and on society. . . . Thus Christians should readily appreciate the need for governments to formulate population policies to safeguard the hope of their peoples for a higher quality of social life and to protect the claims and needs of future generations. The right, indeed duty, of governments to bring home to their people the implications of population trends is accepted.[6]

When a right is curtailed—the right to have as many children as one might want—the social and individual benefits to be accrued should be understood and perceived by those giving up the individual freedom.

Effective Choice as a Human Right

One more aspect of the human rights issue should be touched upon. The United Nations, first in the Tehran Declaration on Human Rights in 1968 and later on numerous other occasions, has declared that it is a basic human right to have the education and means to freely determine the number and spacing of children.

Most emphasis is put on the individual right of choice involved, but there are important political rights proclaimed here also. Nothing is more liberating for the lives of women than to be able to plan their own fertility. Governments should not inhibit information and access to means that make that liberation possible; yet many governments continue to do so. Some still want to force women to produce more babies, as in Eastern Europe; so they forbid abortion and restrict family-planning services. Some forbid contraceptive distribution and use entirely. Access to abortion is still the subject of intense controversy in our own country.

Lack of means and choice is a form of coercion too.

Should not the United States and the United Nations begin to take this matter seriously as a human right?

The ethical questions are indeed difficult ones in the area of population. Some involve us directly, here in the United States. Some we need to face because they will be raised in programs that we support through international agencies, our aid programs, and contributions to churches and voluntary humanitarian organizations. Have we thought enough about our responsibilities? Should we not at least be raising and discussing these questions?

The fundamental bedrock on which population programs must rest is the aim of enhancing life for individuals and for the human community. We must remember the voice that put our responsibility plainly: Whatever you did unto my brothers and sisters here, you did unto me.

CHAPTER 8

Policies and Programs: The U.S. Role

Is there any way an individual in the United States can affect a global issue such as the population problem? Granted that we should be aware of the dangers inherent in continued rapid population growth, granted that we should be concerned about the ethical choices facing policy-makers: Is there really any way that an individual can help determine how soon and in what manner the world achieves population stabilization? Without question, the answer is yes.

There are a surprising number of public policy issues that can make a difference in this area, and the individual joining other concerned individuals always has options for helping to shape public-policy decisions. In this chapter we will look briefly at a number of these population issues.

Development Assistance

Probably any reader of this book can reel off, at a moment's notice, assorted criticisms that have been made of foreign aid. From one side come the charges that it is a huge give-away program that has earned us little gratitude from Third World recipients. Far from being a giveaway, the fact is that about three out of four dollars earmarked for bilateral assistance in 1977 were spent for technical know-how, services, products, and commodities in this country. Much of the economic assistance is in the form of loans, not grants. Further, the United States is eleventh among developed nations in percentage of the gross national product devoted to assistance programs.

From the other side come charges that aid has been a way of dumping food surplus and building U.S. markets rather than of helping people; that most aid has been military and the economic assistance has been used as a political weapon (during the Vietnam war most food aid went to Vietnam to free its own funds for war uses); that programs have fostered dependency rather than helped real development in the poor nations; that aid has actually supported the elite in poor countries.

So unpopular is foreign aid, it is said, that it simply has no real constituency in this country.

The U.S. development assistance program was really launched in 1947 with the Marshall Plan which worked to rehabilitate Western Europe after the war. At its peak, this program received almost 3 percent of the U.S. gross national product. With the economic recovery of Europe, Truman's Point Four program shifted emphasis to assisting the newly emerging nations. Flushed with the success of the Marshall Plan, planners assumed that with the application of moderate economic assistance the developing nations would soon reach a take-off point from which they could move forward on their own.

During the succeeding years, various theories of development took the ascendancy. The somewhat chastening experience of these years showed that we really know very little about how development takes place and how to assist intentionally in making it happen.

Criticism has too often implied that failed efforts were due to bad motives. Richard Dickinson, in discussing difficulties of church development efforts in working with government agencies or governments, said:

On the other hand, there is something clearly distasteful about the presumption of governmental incompetence or malevolence. In many respects, it simply is not true. That argument is too moralistic, not taking ambiguity and ignorance into account. What is more distressing, however, is that simplistic criticism and disdain of governmental and international efforts lead so easily into unwarranted self-righteousness and triumphalism on the part of the churches and individual Christians.[1]

In 1973 came a major revision in U.S. development assistance programs. Congress, urged by church groups among others, mandated a "new directions" approach that placed primary emphasis on direct help for the poor in developing countries. Bilateral programs, through which this approach is implemented, cover areas of food production, rural development and nutrition, population planning and health, and education and human resources. Congress added language stressing the use of appropriate technologies, which can be used on the small farm or the village level, and mandating that women had to be included in development planning and programming.

This act is the major source of U.S. population work abroad. Specific criticism of these efforts has been that our population programs are too "hardware-oriented"—that is, some AID officials seemed to believe that if we could just ship enough condoms and pills around the world, the population problem would be ended. Now the legislation insists on a broader perspective, and recently AID personnel have been directed to give attention to how the other areas of assistance, health and education programs for example, may also have an impact on lowering the fertility rate.

In spite of the greater enthusiasm generated by the "new directions," the level of funding remains low. In 1977, only about 2.31 billion went for bilateral assistance. Since the present U.S. effort is so small and world need is so great, since we really know so little about how constructive change comes about, is there really much point to a development assistance program at all?

Rafael Salas, speaking of population assistance, points out that while external aid has all along been a small fraction of total developmental resources, it can have an effect out of proportion to its size. "Like an extra pulley in a block and tackle in the right place, its strength is multiplied."[2] Further, small projects can often serve as models that can then be replicated on a much larger scale.

There are those who think fundamental changes in world trade and monetary systems are far more important to world development. The question is whether such adjustments are more or less likely to come if the United States were to end its assistance programs, particularly the bilateral ones.

Studies by the World Bank and the Overseas Development Council have estimated that the basic need for food, clothing, shelter, basic health care and education for the world's poor could be met in the next two decades—if the affluent nations would furnish assistance of around 15 billion dollars a year, to be matched by major internal changes within the poor countries themselves to focus on the needs of the majority of their peoples. That would mean increasing current U.S. efforts to perhaps 6 billion dollars a years, still a tiny fraction of our income and budget.[3]

The development assistance program is an important handle on world development, both as substance and symbol. Citizen groups can help to monitor the new directions and can help to shape needed new initiatives. Above all, if there is any hope for increased funding, it will come about only through an informed, active constituency working toward that end. The church constituency, with its long history of concern for human welfare and its strong educational and mission channels seems a natural to be a basic element of that active constituency.

Immigration

"Give me your tired, your poor, your huddled masses yearning to be free." This image of the United States as a haven for the poor who want to work for a better life and for those oppressed for political or religious beliefs has long been a key element of our national mythology—our vision of what we want and believe our nation to be.

While we are indeed a nation of immigrants, the words on the Statue of Liberty have been inaccurate for some time. Nevertheless, the United States still has one of the more liberal immigration policies in the world, and about 400,000 legal immigrants come into the country each year. With the current low birthrates, about 20 percent of our population growth each year comes from this immigration source. Advocates of population stabilization point out that we will never reach zero population growth unless (1) the number of those immigrating is equal to the number of those emigrating from the country each year and the fertility rate is at replacement level (about 2.1 children per woman), or (2) the fertility rate is below replacement level, thus allowing for some immigration. Still, there are few who are seriously recommending that we end all legal immigration because of the emotional wrench that would be caused by such a break with America's past.

The question of legal immigration may loom larger in the future. What is getting intense political scrutiny and increasing publicity now is the matter of illegal immigration. No one is sure just how many illegal immigrants there are in the United States, with estimates ranging from 2 to 12 million. In 1977, 1 million illegals were apprehended, but that does not reveal how many were successful in disappearing into the society without being caught.

Among all the other social and economic effects from legal and illegal immigration, there could be major demographic ones. Zero Population Growth has done projections that show enormous differences in our population in the year 2025 if illegal immigration continues at a high rate. They estimate continued immigration at current levels would mean the need to create an additional 22.8 million jobs between 1976 and 2020.

Although illegal immigrants come from all around the world, chief sources are Mexico, Colombia, Canada, El Salvador, Dominican Republic, Jamaica, and Ecuador. Except for Canada, these nations are all marked by high population growth rates, high unemployment rates, and a high percentage (44%) of their population under fifteen years old.

The issue has become an emotional one on both sides of the U.S.–Mexican border. Here, some Hispanic Americans say they are already a target of harassment, as zealous enforcement officers fail to discriminate between citizens and noncitizens. They fear that proposed laws that would impose penalities on employers who hire illegal aliens might make it more difficult for any Hispanic to be hired, as employers choose to play extra safe. One solution to that problem is some sort of national identification card, which brings shivers to minorities and civil libertarians, fearing it could be used in many repressive ways to control citizens.

There is little agreement on the effects here of the illegal immigration. Some claim they serve our economy by performing necessary menial jobs Americans will not do. Others claim they take many kinds of jobs, thus making much worse our unemployment problems and that they cost the economy billions of dollars in extra social services and in money sent out of the country.

There is equal lack of agreement on solutions to the problem. In addition to the proposal to fine those who employ illegal immigrants, there are proposals to grant a moratorium to those who have been here for some time, while greatly intensifying the effort to prevent the entry of additional ones.

What is certain is that the problem is not going away. Again, solution to poverty/development problems may well be the only long-term answer. But what of the short-term? Since issues of justice are so clearly raised in all aspects of the immigration problem, churches and community groups should be seeking information, discussing, trying to formulate answers, for Congress will surely be forced to act within the next few years.

Family-Planning Services and Contraceptive Research Act

The family-planning program initiated by Congress in 1970 may well be one of the most successful national health programs in our history. The goal of the legislation is to bring family-planning services to all low- and marginal-income women, giving them the same kind of choices in this area that women with access to private physicians have. A recently published study estimates that between 1970 and 1975, the clinic program assisted low- and marginal-income persons to avert 1,098,000 unintended births and teenagers to avert an additional 266,000. Between 4 and 4½ million women are now being served, bringing into their lives the liberating force of being able to plan the number and spacing of their children.[4] Infant and maternal mortality has been reduced, and the emotional and physical well-being of persons of low income has been enhanced.

There are few who would now question the great value and success of the programs initiated under this legislation. Yet between 1973 and 1977, funding levels were virtually frozen. There are still some estimated 3 million women wishing family-planning services who do not have access to them. The impact of an unplanned and unwanted pregnancy can be devastating and can make it more difficult to break the poverty cycle.

This is an ongoing program that needs continuing public support. Congress needs to be urged to fund these efforts at whatever level is needed each year to bring family-planning information, counseling, and services to all who need and desire them.

Under the same legislation, funds are appropriated for the United States' work on contraceptive research. It is possible that the U.S. could make its greatest contribution to the world population effort through work to develop safer, more effective, inexpensive contraceptives that could be used in various social and health situations.

Concern about the effects of long-term use of the pill are rising; yet there is little in view to take its place. Other methods have physical or psychological drawbacks. These fears may be part of the reason behind the rapidly rising rate of sterilization, but as long as this procedure is irreversible, it cannot be of help to younger people who have not yet completed their family.

Current spending for fundamental biological research, contraceptive development, contraceptive evaluation, behavioral research, totaled only 65.3 million dollars for 1978. (In contrast, expenditures on agricultural research rose from about 1.3 billion dollars in 1959 to 3.8 billion in 1974, in constant dollars.)

The Ford Foundation sponsored a review of the state of reproductive research throughout the world, conducted by 160 experts in 26 nations. The report noted:

Whether one's perspective is limited to the personal effects of high fertility on individuals and families or its aggregate effects on nations and the world community, improved regulation of fertility and the expected reduction in fertility levels are urgent objectives in both industrial and developing nations.[5]

The scientists went on to point out that private industry is unlikely to put a major effort into this field because of increasing costs and risks. This means that if new methods are to become available, government research will have to take the lead. The scientific study concluded that world expenditures urgently need to be tripled. This would mean expenditures from all sources in the United States of 328 million dollars in 1980, far above the level likely to be recommended by the Administration or appropriated by Congress. Male contraceptives, long-term contraceptives, reversible sterilization, are among the areas needing greatly increased attention.

Virtually every individual is affected by developments in this area, as are the national and world communities. Here again, the church constituency, through its concern for human welfare—for women being able to make choices, for families achieving greater stability, for children being wanted and healthy—should find support for a greater emphasis on contraceptive and fertility behavioral research, a practical and effective means for expressing that concern.

Teen-age Pregnancy

Most of us would find quite appropriate the efforts in developing nations to raise the age of marriage in order to encourage later and fewer pregnancies. Most Americans would probably be surprised to learn, however, that the childbearing rate of adolescents in the United States is one of the highest in the world. Nearly one in five births here is to a teen-ager. One-fourth of all women aged twenty in 1974 had had at least one child. In 1974, over six hundred thousand teen-agers gave birth, almost thirteen thousand of them under fifteen. Twenty percent of all births to teen-agers were the second or higher order births. The National Center for Health Statistics estimates that nearly half of all teen-age marriages break up within five years. Those which came about as a result of pregnancy are three times more likely to break up.[6]

Small wonder, then, that adolescent pregnancies have been called "an epidemic" that the nation needs urgently to do something about.

This is not only a serious national problem; for the individual it can be a real tragedy. Teen-age health risks are higher, and infant mortality for children born to mothers under fifteen is more than twice as high as for mothers in their early twenties. Financial problems are the norm, and education is usually disrupted. Planned Parenthood of New York City reported in one survey that of two hundred teen-agers who gave birth before age seventeen and elected to keep their babies, 50 percent were on public welfare six years after the birth; an additional 30 percent were barely getting by economically.

In our sex-saturated—and contraceptive-saturated, one would think—society, the stark fact is that only one in five sexually active teen-aged women uses contraception consistently, and of those who do not use it, 70 percent think they cannot become pregnant. The existence of the pill has led many teen-aged males to ignore the issue entirely, leaving the whole responsibility to the girl.

Movies, books, advertisements, television programs, songs in our society, are all full of sexual innuendos, pushing toward physical intercourse. How many countervailing forces can we name that speak of responsible sex to the teen-ager, of sexuality in the total picture of relationship, of commitment and values?

Dr. Sol Gordon of the Institute for Family Research and

Education at Syracuse points out that research findings may be taken as normative when presented baldly.

If we provide statistics showing that there has been a substantial increase in the percentage of teenage women who had had two or more partners, we need to place the statistics in a broader perspective so that we do not leave the impression that something is wrong with a person who is not "with it" and sleeping with more than one partner. We need to talk about the quality of relationships, about love instead of only about sex.[7]

For too long, we have almost idealized our sex activities. As Gordon says, "We have lent credence to the curious kind of turn-on in which a body part substitutes for the whole person." Church and community groups are ideal forums for reenergizing discussions of the goals of our society and of the challenges and opportunities for contributing to the welfare of all in an interdependent world. All of which may seem far afield of the subject of youthful sexuality, but the whole person is what needs to be addressed.

Abortion

When abortions were all performed illegally in this country, Alan Guttmacher said that they constituted the third largest racket in the United States, coming only after gambling and narcotics.[8] The cost in suffering and death for women was untold; yet the problem was largely ignored for years.

In 1973, the Supreme Court ruled that abortion should be a decision between a doctor and his patient during the first trimester of pregnancy. The state could have health regulations during the second trimester and could forbid abortion entirely after that. The Court held that questions such as when life begins are basically theological, and with no consensus among theologians or religions regarding them, the questions are therefore not proper subjects for law.

Many thought the question of legal abortion had been settled, giving access to medically safe abortions to those who desired them, leaving those who opposed them on moral ground free to teach and preach against abortion. Instead, the battle has escalated. At every level of government—local, state, national—public-policy battles rage ever more fiercely as those opposed to abortion seek to restrict or eliminate access to it.

Much effort has gone into seeking passage of a constitutional amendment forbidding abortion—some versions excepting abortion done to save the life of the mother, some declaring that the fetus, from the moment of conception, should have full civil rights. One of the continuing and hardest-fought battles centers on the use of Medicaid funds for abortion. Opponents claim their tax money should not be used to pay for something morally repugnant to them. Congress proved very sympathetic to this argument, seeming to forget that all taxpayers pay for things they consider immoral or unethical—arms sales, tobacco price supports, military assistance to dictators, for example. Medicaid's purpose, however, was to equalize health care between those who could pay for private services and those too poor to do so. Excluding payment for abortion for poor women is simple discrimination; for they too may face contraceptive failure or the prospect of bearing an infant with severe genetic deficiencies or pregnancy at the age of forty-five, or any of the other sad reasons that impel women to seek abortions.

Most major Protestant and Jewish groups have taken the stance that abortion should be legally available, that the moral questions should be a matter of the woman's conscience and the churches' teachings. Because those upholding the right to abortion have found this a difficult and emotional matter to speak out on, it has often seemed that *the* religious position must be against abortion.

In response to this situation, over one hundred Christian and Jewish ethicists in September, 1977, issued a "Call to Concern," which said in part:

"Pro-life" must not be limited to concern for the unborn; it must also include a concern for the duality of life as a whole. The affirmation of life in Judeo-Christian ethics requires a commitment to make life healthy and whole from beginning to end. Considering the best medical advice, the best moral insight, and a concern for the total quality of the whole life cycle for the born and the unborn, we believe that abortion may in some instances be the most loving act possible.

We call upon the leaders of religious groups supporting abortion rights to speak out more clearly and publicly in response to the dangerously increasing influence of the absolutist position.

The move to legalize abortion has been spreading worldwide. Were the right now lost here, the impact could have horrifying ramifications for the lives of women and families everywhere.

A U.S. Population Policy

Since the ill-fated report of the Commission on Population Growth and the American Future in 1972, there has been little attention to any need for a coherent U.S. population policy. Many Americans think we have already reached zero population growth in this country; so it would seem to be a puzzling time to suggest that we need an official population policy. How might a population policy be useful?

⁂ It would help us to be more intentional about our population goals. The United States has not stabilized its population but rather it is still growing by over 1 million persons a year.

Few things are harder to predict with certainty than fertility behavior. We can't be sure of the reasons the birthrate went so high during the fifties—nor why it has fallen so low in the seventies. The fact that many young women have been marrying later and postponing having children may account for the recent low fertility rate. Now it is edging up again. The number of children today's young women (a large group because of the baby boom of the fifties) decide to have before they end their childbearing is a momentous decision.

As a nation, we need to be discussing what our population goals should be and involving young people in those discussions. Do we have any values threatened by continually increasing population? What is the approximate size of population we think would be ideal for this country? What are the implications for childbearing and for immigration in such a total?

A special congressional committee has been looking into all the aspects of population behavior and growth, but most of the American public know little about it, in spite of the importance of this for our future. A national debate on population goals could help us sort out these questions and help us to move more deliberately toward the population size we think would be most life enhancing.

⁎⁎ A population policy would give us a framework for considering interrelated problems. Employment continues to be one of our thorniest problems closely tied in with demographic factors. Often we seem not to relate our growing problems of inflation, of land and water, of pollution and energy to the numbers of our people and the world's people. Clearly, they all need to be looked at in relation to one another and on a national basis.

⁎⁎ A population policy would help us adjust to demographic change. Much of the dynamism and innovation in our economic development has been fueled by our growing population. The prospect of near-static growth creates panic in some minds. They picture an aging society, bereft of ideas and energy, with business declining and social institutions rigidified. Population stability will certainly be a new situation and will create new challenges, but there is no reason to assume it has to be a darker future. It can mean lessened pressures for increasing consumption and continual economic growth, lower crime rates, more leisure time.

*** A U.S. population policy would be an important symbol to the rest of the world. In 1974, the United States joined other nations in signing the Plan of Action which recommended that each nation consider adopting a population policy that would set goals for population size and the programs needed to achieve them. Since then, we have been active in promoting policies for others but have done almost nothing to implement this for ourselves.

Our influence, for good or ill, is immense—not only economically and militarily but socially (trends) and culturally (mores) also. A national consensus on the need for and adoption of a population policy could help other nations to take similar steps. It would add to our credibility that we are serious about dealing not only with population but with poverty, resource use, pollution.

Individual Action Can Help

Population growth is an enormous global problem, a force that almost defies reckoning. Yet actually it is a situation with many possibilities for action by the individual American citizen. Through all the public-policy issues covered here—development assistance, family-planning services and contraceptive research, abortion—there are practical means of helping individuals, the community, the world. All it takes is a serious commitment to do something rather than just to talk, to acquire the skills to make an impact on the political process, and to enlist other like-minded individuals.

The World Council of Churches' statement on population declares, "The Christian understanding of quality of life, in relation to population policies, means the enrichment of personal, family and social life—what Jesus called 'having life more abundantly.' " If our goal is assisting all to have that more abundant life, nothing less than an active participation in these issues will serve.

CHAPTER 9

Putting You and Me
in the Global Picture

For every complex problem, there is a simple solution—
and it is wrong. H. L. Mencken's wry comment is a useful
warning for us as we look at the complex of interrelated
global problems we face today. There are no simple
solutions, but there are steps we can begin to take today.
This book started out with the personal dimensions of the
population problem. And, after looking at the many
national and international aspects of population growth,
we end on the note of personal responsibility for moving
toward solutions.

There are skills we can acquire to become effective in
public policy. Perhaps even more important, there are
societal and attitudinal changes that must occur and that we
must assist in coming if we are to face the very different
future with courage, with hope, and even with eager
anticipation.

Let us look first a bit more closely at the public-policy
action possibilities. In the preceeding chapter, we looked at
some of the issues in which citizen action is needed and can
be effective: development assistance; family-planning
services and contraceptive research; immigration; teen-age
pregnancy, abortion, a national population policy.

A few interested individuals is all the nucleus you need to
begin working. Start by arranging an event that will
stimulate interest in population issues. Perhaps a seminar

on why women have babies (material is available from the United Methodist Department of Population, 100 Maryland Avenue NE, Washington, D.C. 20002). Or perhaps a panel on how soon we should aim for zero population growth—and how do we get there. Contact local chapters of Zero Population Growth, Friends of the Earth, Sierra Club, and Planned Parenthood for information and speakers. A nearby college probably has numerous students from Third World nations who could tell your group about their own national policies.

Whatever program you choose, the kickoff event should be lively and informative, and end with a definite next step to which people can commit themselves. Though you may enlist a number of people who are interested in population issues in general (after your provocative first program!), it will be wise to keep your focus quite narrow, at least at the beginning. Look over the possible areas for action, choose one, agree on an overall goal that the whole group finds feasible and challenging, and then set one or more specific action goals. For example, you might choose as your goal: increased funding for the development assistance program; and your immediate action goal might be: to secure the vote of Congressperson X and Senators Y and Z for more funds in the development assistance act this year.

Plan your strategy carefully, ask each participant to accept a specific assignment, and be realistic in what can be expected. That will do much to guarantee continued interest and participation. Keep the structure as informal as possible; there are few people around who want to get involved in a new organization with bylaws, elections, too many meetings. The issue is the thing, not the organization. Keep informal notes on your meetings, to have a record of decisions and activities, but don't make it a chore. One person can simply keep the record, which all can refer to if necessary.

You may continually spark the interest of others—and you hope you will—so that new people may show up each time. Don't let each get-together get bogged down in rehashing what has gone on before, a quick way of killing interest in any project. Set aside fifteen minutes to bring new people on board, and then move ahead.

A lack of formal organizational structure and small numbers does not mean you will be ineffective. You can join other groups that are interested in the same goals, and you can use clever ideas to gain the attention of your church, your community, and the media. For example, when the state legislature is working on abortion legislation don't simply ask for contributions for the lobbying effort. Ask various churches or groups or clubs to "buy a bus" to go to the Capitol for lobbying. It may be easier to raise one hundred dollars for a specific task like that—and should help to fill the buses also. Be sure everyone associated with your cause wears a flower, a ribbon, a button—some identifying mark that shows to people in the corridors as well as those whom you are seeking that there is a concerned group of citizens all working together.

All you need is the desire to be effective on political issues. There are many groups eager to help you acquire the skills: groups such as League of Women Voters, Zero Population Growth, Women's National Political Caucus, to mention only a few. The Religious Coalition for Abortion Rights will help on that issue. The social action agencies of each denomination have much helpful information. Check the Appendix to this book for listings of organizations that will offer help in various policy areas.

Local Service Activities

Perhaps your nucleus of concerned people will decide they are more interested in a local service activity. A church could be a natural and reassuring place for a teen counseling center on responsible sexuality, a place where they could get answers to their questions from caring, supportive adults. There are churches that serve their communities by lending their facilities for provision of family-planning services as well as counseling. By enlisting a few doctors and nurses to donate a few hours a week plus volunteers, a church can help with family planning for people in inner cities, rural communities, and so forth. Or a church group might offer to provide transportation for women with small children to enable them to go to a family-planning clinic elsewhere.

A church would be an excellent center for looking into sterilization practices in the area. If there is a local public hospital, find out what the sterilization regulations are. If they are so restrictive that people who want sterilization cannot obtain the service, that would require one kind of campaign. The group could also see that guidelines to protect women against abuse are strictly observed.

Beyond the specific policy areas in which people can take helpful action, there are fundamental societal and attitudinal changes we could assist to make the passage into the strange world of the future less painful and wrenching. Someone has said that technological change somehow is always seen as progress, while social change is viewed—at least at first—as retrogressive or decadent. We always yearn for the certainties of our own time, even though we know that change is inevitable. The changes facing us in the next few decades will almost surely represent a break sharper than what has occurred for a very long time. Said columnist George Will:

If growth is becoming more difficult to sustain, we may be entering a period of unprecedented testing of the American dream. That in itself represents a change in the American condition. We have for some time been more confident of the future and of ourselves than we are likely to be again in the foreseeable future.[1]

During the last twenty-five years, world fuel consumption tripled, oil and gas consumption tripled, and electricity use grew almost sevenfold. Americans currently consume more than one-third of the entire world's production of oil and must now import nearly 100 percent of many of the materials deemed essential for an industrial society. We know such trends in growth cannot be sustained indefinitely. Says Denis Hayes, "Nature abhors exponential curves as well as vacuums."

So our nation has begun to struggle with the necessity of slowing the rate of use of resources, but with little success so far. We know that most Europeans live well on half as much energy as we consume on the average. Most of us would admit that our happiness has not tripled as our energy consumption has. Many have come to accept the idea that more is not better forever. When people have had to carry water from a stream, having a well dug near the house is a tremendous step forward. When clean and sanitary water is piped into the house, it unquestionably adds greatly to comfort and well-being. When a five-speed shower nozzle is acquired as the latest gadget, it is decidedly marginal in its contribution to increased human welfare. In fact, many gadgets become nuisances in their maintenance and storage problems. Yet, we don't know how to turn off this push for consumption. We are fearful that many jobs will be lost if we change our energy-gorging, gadget-buying ways. Like Scarlett O'Hara, we know that something terrible may have happened, but we prefer to think about it tomorrow.

In setting forth "Why We Need to Get Poor Quick," writer Tom Bender says:

This is a fundamental and permanent change in our condition that even our wildest dreams of fusion power and unlimited energy cannot alter. Even if such dreams should prove technically possible, they would only move the timetable back a few years until we have to meet the same unrealities of infinite growth in a finite world, with a larger population and closer to the absolute limits of our planet.[2]

Is all this taking us afield of the population question? Not at all. Lester Brown of Worldwatch Institute has estimated that the annual increase in consumption of goods and services is rather equally divided between population growth and rising individual affluence. As we have seen, our population is still growing, as is our rate of consumption. The same is true for most of the rest of the world.

In today's climate, it is easy to be both cynical and pessimistic. Countering this is one fundamental contribution we can make in this unfolding challenge: saying with Paul, "Let hope keep you joyful." All futures are unknown and uncertain. As a nation we do face a time of testing and also a time of unparalleled opportunity. There is more serious talk today of how to bring about greater equity between the nations and within nations than perhaps there has ever been. Lester Brown suggests that "what we may witness is the emergence of a situation in which it will be in the interest of the rich countries to launch a concerted attack on global poverty in order to reduce the threat to our future well-being posed by continuing population growth."

We have seen that the move to smaller family sizes started with people, not with governments or institutions. Again, a people's movement could lead to new definitions of what constitutes the good life, based on family pleasures; intellectual, spiritual, and communal values rather than on consumption. Patterns of life could include new mixtures of paid employment, voluntary service, education, and recreation. Thus the specter of massive unemployment and a declining economy could give way to a reality of productive roles for all, with the added excitement of changing roles at different times of life.

In practical terms, we may find that we create thousands of new repair/maintenance jobs by making things last instead of by throwing them away. As natural resources grow more expensive (as they grow scarcer), we may once again accord dignity to the application of human energy to tasks. It could become common for couples to share jobs and child-nurturing tasks.

There is now much testing and unease about women's and men's roles in our families and our societies. There are those who play on fears by promising a return to happiness if only the female will be totally submissive to the male. They imply that change can be kept at bay, and all will be well. This ignores the fact that social and economic forces have been causing fundamental shifts in the lives and roles of women. When human survival was at stake, a woman needed to do nothing more than produce children to make a clear contribution to humankind. (Of course, women were always contributing much more but usually derived little status from other contributions.) When economic growth, technological advancement, civilization itself seemed dependent on growing populations, a woman could feel fulfilled and important by having a large family.

Human survival still depends on a women having an average of 2.1 children; but beyond that, childbearing may be a threat rather than a contribution. In the modern, industrialized society, women have become largely consumers not producers, and that is not a totally satisfying role in life. This basic change cannot be glossed over by any number of "total-woman" movements.

Women as well as men want lives that are productive; yet women have long been barred from equal participation in realms of life beyond the home. Thus we have today's movement for liberation and equality, and though the specific forms may vary, it is clearly a worldwide movement. In the United States, much of the energy has focused on passage of the equal rights amendment. The language is simple: Equality of rights under the law shall not be denied or abridged by the United States or by any state on account of sex. It is hard to believe that opponents are in favor of the opposite: Inequality of rights based on sex shall be enforced under the law. The vehemence, therefore, must stem from fear of change and a belief that if only the ERA can be defeated, the future can be held at bay, and an idealized past will return. So the ERA has become an important symbol, but whether the amendment is passed or not, change in the basic requirements of women's lives has dictated that the push for equality, and new ways of contributing, will continue.

Women, men, and children need help in this time of changing attitudes and roles, and churches should be a caring center were questions can be dealt with openly and with care for all.

Another element needs to be included in this look at reassessed attitudes. The idea of responsible parenthood has long been the ideal held up by churches, within a changing context of just what those words mean. "Responsible parenthood," said Fagley, "in the context of the population explosion more often than not means restricted or limited procreation in view of the total responsibility of parenthood. It is more than a euphemism for family planning or birth control. It implies a basically affirmative attitude toward procreation."[3]

Now it may be important to add the concept of "intentional parenting." In early days of the Christian Church, celibacy was held the more perfect state of being; but for those not capable of it, marriage implied the duty of parenthood. Anyone who would deliberately choose to not have children was branded as abnormal or selfish or hedonistic. This is still largely true. It is pretty much assumed that marriage implies having children, just fewer of them.

If that assumption continues to be the norm, and if there is a need for population stabilization, we face a future of couples and children (2.1 of them) marching by pairs like residents of Noah's ark in an endless line to the future. Achieving that average, however, could mean a variety of family sizes if we create an atmosphere in which people are free to choose, without social onus, to remain unmarried, or married and childless, or married with different numbers of children.

To do that, children and young poeple would have to become accustomed to the idea that being parents is something you deliberately choose and prepare yourself for and not just a condition that inevitably happens. The National Organization for Non-Parents has a brochure for young people entitled "Am I Parent Material?" Its introduction says: "If you decide to have a child, it'll be a decision that will affect you for the rest of your life. Think about it. Taking responsibility for a new life is awesome. . . . You *do* have a choice." If we think about it, this is still a pretty radical idea in our society; yet it is one whose time has surely come. The need for every couple to produce many offspring is no longer valid. Has not the time come, instead, for us to encourage "intentional parenting"?

This certainly does not imply any lessening in love for children but rather a serious communal commitment to the well-being of all children so that all can be involved in nurturing whether or not they have children of their own.

As Dean Philip Wogaman has said, "Acknowledging that too large a population actually frustrates God's loving purpose need not detract from our love of people or our recognition of God's love of people."[4]

Yet how much more difficult it is going to be to maintain the preciousness of the individual life in a world of 8, 9, 10 billion people, more than twice as many as the world holds today. Think back to the first winter the Pilgrims spent in New England. Then, each death—and there were many— was a true crisis for the community. Bodies were buried at night and graves concealed so that the Indians would not suspect how pitifully few were the remnant. Today in our country we scarcely give a thought to the over fifty thousand deaths each year from automobile accidents, and many find it outrageous that car speed should be curbed, even to save tens of thousands of lives a year.

We have never done too good a job of living up to the Christian ideal of love for fellow human beings, but how much harder it will be as numbers swell and swell. When one hundred thousand people can die in one tidal wave and their numbers be replaced in less than thirty days, can we seriously believe in the transcendent value of every human life? We must. Difficult as it is for us to hold on to that belief, to let it diminish or die opens up a world in which any act is not only possible but proper to control numbers in the name of stability, security, and survival. Christ said, "Whatever you have done for the least of these, you have done unto me." He told us that even the hairs of the head of each person are numbered by God. Christians and others of like belief must take as their primary population task safeguarding the belief that the tiny one has value in the midst of the teeming billions.

What does the future hold for population growth? No one really knows. Even the greatest experts in the field do not know exactly how many people there are in the world nor how fast their numbers are growing. Much of the recent hope that the birthrate is falling significantly is based on

China—and no one can be sure of the facts in that vast country, including the Chinese. Other claims of success are based on a few small nations, and success is defined as bringing growth rates down a few percentage points, not in reaching population stabilization.

World population is still growing at probably 1.7 percent a year. We know that rate cannot continue very much longer, and we know that there will be many more people in the world before essential stabilization is reached. Population policy must take account of both factors. Some years ago, historian Arnold Toynbee in a lecture on population and the food supply asked: "What is the true end of humankind? Is it to populate the Earth with the maximum number of human beings that can be kept alive? Or is it to enable human beings to lead the best kind of life that the spiritul limitations of human nature allow?" His answer was that "living human beings, whatever their number, shall develop the highest capacities of their nature. . . . What we should aim at is the optimum size of the population for this purpose in the economic and social circumstances of each succeeding generation."

People in balance with resources, resources equitably available, opportunities to develop their human capacities available to all: Is not that the kind of world we hope for? We need to look unafraid at the problems and the prospects, and then undergird our hopes with action. Population is people—you and me and several billion others, all of us existing and striving in the same world. There is no separate future for rich and poor.

NOTES

CHAPTER 1

1. Richard M. Fagley, *The Population Explosion and Christian Responsibility* (New York: Oxford University Press, 1960), p. 192.
2. Ernest Havemann and the editors of Time-Life Books, *Birth Control* (New York: Time, Inc., 1967), p. 22.
3. Quoted in ibid., p. 13.
4. Dom Moraes, *A Matter of People* (New York: Praeger Publishers, 1974), p. 124.
5. Fagley, *The Population Explosion and Christian Responsibility,* p. 9.

CHAPTER 2

1. Lester R. Brown, *The Twenty-Ninth Day* (New York: W. W. Norton & Co., 1978), p. 113.
2. Lester R. Brown, "The Urban Prospect: Reexamining the Basic Assumptions," *Population and Development Review* (June 1976), p. 268.
3. Brown, *The Twenty-Ninth Day,* p. 171.
4. *Employment, Growth and Basic Needs: A One-World Problem,* prepared by the International Labor Office (New York: Praeger Publishers, 1977), p. 3.
5. Richard Heilbroner, *An Inquiry into the Human Prospect* (New York: W. W. Norton & Co., 1974).

CHAPTER 3

1. William J. Robinson, *Sexual Problems of Today* (New York: The Critic and Guide Company, 1912), p. 86.
2. Emily Taft Douglas, *Margaret Sanger: Pioneer of the Future* (New York: Holt, Rinehart and Winston, 1970), p. 105 ff.

3. Richard Symonds and Michael Carder, *The United Nations and the Population Question* (New York: McGraw-Hill Book Co., 1973), p. 103.
4. Phyllis Tilson Piotrow, *World Population Crisis: The United States Response* (New York: Praeger Publishers, 1973), p. 34.
5. Ibid., p. 17.
6. *Population and the American Future,* the Report of the Commission on Population Growth and the American Future, (U.S. Government Printing Office), No. 5258-0002, p. 12.

CHAPTER 4

1. Terence H. Hull, Valerie J. Hull, and Singarimbun, *Indonesia's Family Planning Story: Success and Challenge.* Population Bulletin, vol. 32 (Washington, D.C.: Population Reference Bureau, 1977).
2. Calman J. Cohen, "Mexico Lays Base for Nationwide Family Planning Program," *Population Dynamics Quarterly,* vol. 1 [Winter 1973] (International Program for Population Analysis, Smithsonian Institution), p. 2.

CHAPTER 5

1. Moraes, *A Matter of People,* p. 6.
2. Statement on National Population Policy, New Delhi, April 16, 1976, *Population and Development Review,* vol. 2 (June 1976), p. 309.
3. "China's Experience in Population Control: The Elusive Model," Prepared for the Committee on Foreign Affairs, U.S. House of Representatives (September 1974), p. 11.

CHAPTER 6

1. Will Durant, *The Age of Faith* (New York: Simon and Schuster, 1950), p. 363.
2. Lester R. Brown, Patricia L. McGrath, and Bruce Stokes, "Twenty-two Dimensions of the Population Problem," *Worldwatch Paper No. 5* (Washington, D.C.: The Worldwatch Institute), p. 9.
3. Perdita Huston, "Power and Pregnancy," *The New Internationalist* (June 1977), p. 10.
4. Huston, "How Free to Choose?" *People,* vol. 4 (1977) p. 4.
5. Moraes, *A Matter of People,* p. 161.
6. "Women, Population and Development," *Population Profiles* 7 (United Nations Fund for Population Activities).

CHAPTER 7

1. Roger L. Shinn, "Religious Communities and Changing Population Attitudes," *The Population Crisis and Moral Responsibility,* ed. J. Philip Wogaman (Washington, D.C.: Public Affairs Press, 1973), p. 300.
2. Drew Christiansen, "Ethics and Compulsory Population Control," *Hastings Center Report* (February 1977), p. 31.
3. Garrett Hardin, "Lifeboat Ethics: The Case Against Helping the Poor," *Psychology Today* (September 1974), p. 40.
4. Allan Rosenfeld, M.D., "The Ethics of Supervising Family Planning in Developing Nations," *Hastings Center Report* (February 1977), p. 26.
5. Christiansen, "Ethics and Population Control," p. 31.
6. "Population Policy, Social Justice, and the Quality of Life, vol. 9, A Report from the World Council of Churches, 1973, p. 2.

CHAPTER 8

1. Richard D. Dickinson, *To Set at Liberty the Oppressed* (Commission on the Churches' Participation in Development, World Council of Churches, 1975), p. 108.
2. Rafael M. Salas, *People: An International Choice* (Oxford: Pergamon Press, 1976), p. 5.
3. Roger D. Hansen, "Major U.S. Options on North-South Relations," *The United States and World Development, Agenda 1977* (New York: 1977), p. 67.
4. *Planned Births: The Future of the Family and the Quality of American Life* (June 1977) (Washington, D.C.: The Alan Guttmacher Institute), p. 7.
5. R. O. Greep, M. A. Koblinsky, and F. S. Jaffe, "Reproduction and Human Welfare: A Challenge to Research." *BioScience* (November 1976), p. 677.
6. *11 Million Teenagers: What Can Be Done About the Epidemic of Adolescent Pregnancies in the United States?* (Washington, D.C.: The Alan Guttmacher Institute, 1977).
7. Sol Gordon and Peter Scales, "The Myth of the Normal Outlet," *Journal of Pediatric Psychology,* vol. 2 (1977), p. 101.
8. Alan Guttmacher, "Who Owns Fertility?" *Sexuality: A Search for Perspective,* ed. Donald L. Grummon and Andrew M. Barclay (New York: Van Nostrand Reinhold Co., 1971), p. 180.

CHAPTER 9

1. George Will, quoted in *The Futurist* (August 1977), p. 210.
2. Tom Bender, "Why We Need to Get Poor Quick," *The Futurist* (August 1977), p. 210.
3. Fagley, *The Population Explosion and Christian Responsibility,* p. 5.
4. J. Philip Wogaman, "The Church and the Population Crisis," *engage magazine* (December 1971), p. 34.

BOOK LIST

Brown, Lester R. *The Twenty-Ninth Day.* New York: W. W. Norton & Co. with Worldwatch Institute, 1978. 363 pp., $3.95.

Ethics for a Crowded World. A seminar series prepared by the Center for Ethics and Social Policy, Graduate Theological Union, Berkeley, California.

Haupt, Arthur, and Kane, Thomas T. *Population Handbook.* Washington, D.C.: The Population Reference Bureau, 1978. 59 pp., $2.

Hessel, Dieter T., ed. *Beyond Survival: Bread and Justice in Christian Perspective.* New York: Friendship Press, 1978. 222 pp., $4.25.

Heilbroner, Robert L. *An Inquiry into the Human Prospect.* New York: W. W. Norton & Co., 1974. 150 pp., $5.95.

Huston, Perdita. *Third World Women Speak Out.* Washington, D.C.: Overseas Development Council, 1978.

McCleary, Paul, and Wogaman, J. Philip. *Quality of Life in a Global Society.* New York: Friendship Press with Church World Service, 1978. 65 pp., $2.50.

Wogaman, J. Philip, ed. *The Population Crisis and Moral Responsibility.* Washington, D.C.: Public Affairs Press and The Population Institute. 340 pp., $7.50.

APPENDIX

Organizations to contact for information and resources

The Alan Guttmacher Institute
515 Madison Avenue
New York, NY 10022
Research and educational materials on adolescent pregnancy and family planning.

Department of Population
United Methodist Board of Church and Society
100 Maryland Avenue NE
Washington, DC 20002
Resources, including workshop materials, specifically for churches. A Population Alert on issues.

Family Life and Population Program
Church World Service
475 Riverside Drive
New York, NY 10027

Office of Population
Agency for International Development
Department of State
Washington, DC 20523

Population Reference Bureau, Inc.
1337 Connecticut Avenue NW
Washington, DC 20036
Publishes many booklets on aspects of population, plus a yearly data sheet.

YOU, ME, AND A FEW BILLION MORE

United Nations Fund for Population Activities
485 Lexington Avenue
New York, NY 10017

Zero Population Growth
1346 Connecticut Avenue NW
Washington, DC 20036
Publishes newsletter and brief resources on special population issues.